My Life in Print

My Life in Print

Donna Hord Hunt

Edited by
Mavis Anne Bryant

DEDICATION

To David

Still the light of my life
After fifty years of marriage
April 2, 1965

ISBN: 1515070697

ISBN-13: 9781515070696

Library of Congress Control Number: [LCCN]

Contents

Fig. 2. Inez Vaughan Hord, Nannie Mathis Vaughan, Anna Hendrix Vaughan, and Donna Hord, ca. 1935.

Illustrations

Figure (continued)

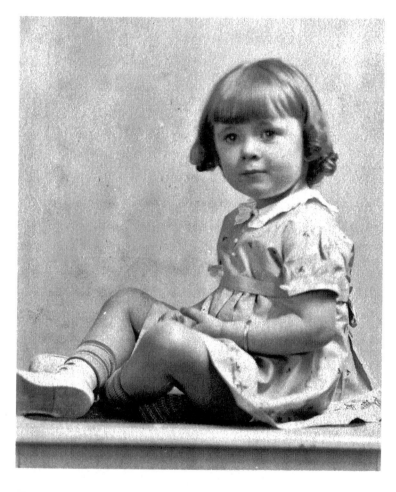

Fig. 3. Donna Hord as a child.

Introduction

Among the newspaper columns that I have been writing for many years in *The Denison Herald*, the *Denison Daily Post*, and the *Herald Democrat*, most have dealt with aspects of the history of Grayson County, Texas. Contrary to what some people may believe, however, sometimes I write about something other than history. This book is a collection of columns recounting my own most vivid experiences and memories. If you like, call it personal history.

My family always has meant the world to me, and I was told many years ago to write about what you know best. My family members now mostly live only as memories, but they are what make me most proud. Most of my memories are wonderful, but as with most families, there are a few that are bittersweet.

Mavis Anne Bryant and I have selected those columns that express some of my feelings and remembrances of the Hunt, Hord, Vaughan, Mathis, Duke, and Hawkins families, as well as my mentor and friends. We have included a biographical sketch for those of you who haven't known me all my life. Mavis, who edited the book, insisted that we include a list of all my columns and some features written since I went to work at *The Denison Herald* in the early 1960s.

Complementing the articles are photographs that take me back to my childhood and recall important events in my adult life. Sorting through my old photos has been a real trip down memory lane. As with the two previous books that Mavis and I wrote together (*Two Schools on Main Street: The Pride of Denison, Texas, 1873-2007*; and *Images of America: Denison*, a pictorial history) and the most recent one that I wrote and Mavis edited (*Frontier Denison, Texas*), it

9

has been a real challenge to pick just the right pictures from our collections.

The most challenging thing about this book has been that some of it was written a number of years ago. Locating newsprint or computerized copies of all these features took many months. After countless hours perusing the Internet and poring over microfilm at the Denison and Sherman public libraries, Mavis filled more than twenty thick three-ring binders with information. Then she edited and designed the book.

It is our hope that the lengthy list of writings in the back of this book, identified by title and date of publication, may be of some benefit to future researchers seeking information on particular topics and people.

Many thanks to John Wright, publisher of the *Herald Democrat*, for allowing me to reproduce the columns that have run in the newspaper. Thanks also to Don Eldredge, retired editor, and Jonathan Cannon, current editor, with whom I have worked during the years my columns have appeared in the newspaper.

My husband of fifty years, David Hunt, has been patient and supportive as always. He acted as my proofreader when the features were originally written and once again as this book was being put together.

A big thank you goes to the readers who have followed my columns and features all these years and to the newcomers to this area who read to learn more about our wonderful section of Texas. Many of you have encouraged me to put my writings in a book; *Frontier Denison, Texas,* and *My Life in Print* have been created in response to those requests.

Donna Hord Hunt
Denison, Texas
July 2015

1

On Mother's Day

It's Mother's Day, and the roses are blooming.

Mother's Day is a time of joy for many—especially those who have recently become mothers for the first time. It can also be a time of sadness for those spending their first Mother's Day without their own mother.

Thirty years ago I began experiencing joyous Mother's Days, but this year it's a day of sadness. Three weeks ago my mother left this earth for a better life beyond.

Though the last several years were not happy, healthy times for her, she left many pleasant memories to be shared by her husband of almost 56 years, her two daughters, her brother, and grandchildren.

When I was growing up, we always had red and white roses on Mother's Day. If our mother was living, the custom was to wear a red rose to church on her day; if she was in heaven, people wore a white rose. Both my grandmothers were very much alive, so my dad went in search of four red roses for my parents, my sister, and me to wear, along with two white roses for my grandmothers to wear. We never seemed to have the right color roses blooming in our yard at the time, so Daddy would drive around, checking out fences and rose bushes blooming in the medians of Main and Woodard streets, where he "borrowed" a few of the beautiful blooming flowers for us to wear. I'm sure he wasn't the only one

11

who did a little scavenger hunt on Mother's Day, because the flowers were very plentiful at church services.

I remember the family dinners that Mother fretted and stewed over but which were prepared to perfection. There were no ready-cooked or deli-bought foods on the menu. Everything was cooked from scratch, all the way to the beautiful coconut cake for dessert. There was always plenty for the Sunday noon meal, then enough for snacking at night. We had to finish everything off that night because Daddy didn't want to eat the leftovers the next week.

I remember the beautiful clothes my mother sewed for me when I was just a child, and how she struggled with the old pedal Singer sewing machine. She thought she was in heaven when she got a new electric model. She had much more patience with sewing than this daughter has, though. I've seen her sit for hours picking out stitches when the garment didn't fit the way she thought it should.

I've seen Mother watching television, talking, reading instructions, and knitting for a half a day at a time without stopping when she was making an afghan, a lovely outfit for herself, or a sweater or dress for a grandchild. We all have something she knitted with love to remember her by.

Mother's interests were her husband, her family, her church, and her home. She never wanted to travel to far-off places, and she was so frightened of water above her ankles that she didn't even particularly like to go to Lake Texoma. She hated to see her grandchildren play in the water. I think she must have had a terrible scare when she was a youngster.

While her circle of activity was mostly within her family, she was proud to see others branch out and accomplish their life goals. She was proud of her younger brother who has been recognized on many levels for his contributions to society, and she was proud of her daughters and the way they raised their families. She loved her grandchildren and great-grandchildren and always asked about them.

Mother and Daddy were as close as two peas in a pod, and now that she's gone, he feels an emptiness that only a person who has lost a mate can imagine.

2

Things Our Mothers Taught Us

It's nostalgic to remember our mothers and the things they did (or tried to) teach us as we were growing up. A friend sent me an article entitled "Remembering Mom's Clothesline." It expressed many of the things my mother practiced every day.

Growing up, we had two iron poles with arms, holding three or four lines of heavy clothesline wire. Because sheets, pants, and large bath towels were so heavy that they would sag and touch the ground, we had a long wooden pole that pushed the wire holding these items up so that they didn't get dirty.

Wash day on Monday was a colorful sight to see around town. Neighbors could get to know neighbors by watching their clotheslines. You could tell when guests were in the house by the appearance of fancy sheets and company tablecloths. You could tell when a new baby had arrived by all the diapers that were hung. Ages of children were pretty evident. If a wash was dingy and gray, that neighbor might be shunned.

There were a few basic rules for hanging clothes on the line. Neighbors kept tabs on when these rules were broken:

- You had to hang the socks by the toes, NOT the top.

- You hung pants by the bottom (cuffs), not the waistband.

- You had to wash the clothesline before hanging any clothes. You walked the entire length of each line with a

13

damp cloth around the lines to be sure they were clean.

- Clothes had to hang in a certain order, with the whites being hung first. Towels were placed all together, sheets together, etc.

- You *never* hung a shirt by the shoulders, always by the tail.

- Hang the sheets and towels on the outside lines, so they would hide your "unmentionables" in the middle. Mothers were aware that there were perverts and busybodies who looked for these things. I was always embarrassed when mine appeared on the line right out there for everyone to see.

- It didn't matter if it was sub-zero weather, clothes would "freeze-dry." If they didn't get completely dry, they were draped over furniture in the house after you bundled up and brought them in to finish drying.

- Always gather the clothespins when you take down dry clothes, because pins left on the lines were "tacky"!

- If you did a little planning, you could line the clothes up so that each item did not need two clothespins, but shared one of the clothespin with the next washed item.

- Clothes had to be off the line before dinnertime, neatly folded in the clothesbasket and ready to be "sprinkled and ironed."

For the younger generation, "sprinkled and ironed" may be a strange term, but in our day, almost every garment we placed on our bodies had to be ironed. Clothes looked best if they were dampened with water by a "sprinkler" (a soda pop bottle with a sprinkler head placed on it) and then put into a sack and left overnight to "dampen" the garments all the way through. This made the hot iron run over them easily, pressing out the wrinkles. Even pillowcases and sometimes sheets, kitchen towels, men's boxer shorts, and other seldom-seen items frequently got the full works.

Today clotheslines are mostly a thing of the past, since dryers are a lot less work and more efficient. But the smell of sheets, towels, and clothes, freshly washed and air-dried outside, is a treasure that we miss. Not enough to go back to our mothers' way, but enough to make us nostalgic when we think about it.

Yes, Mother's Day is a time of sadness for this family and a lot of other families the world over who have experienced the same type of loss. But as we read the "Births" column in today's newspaper and see all the families celebrating this Mother's Day with a new member, we realize that this is all part of God's plan.

We can only be grateful that we were alive to be a part of this lovely lady's life.

Fig. 4. Nancy Elizabeth "Lizzie" Duke Hawkins, Nannie Evelyn Hawkins Hord Davis, Lucious R. Hord, and baby Donna Hord, ca. 1938.

Fig. 5. Donna Hord pinning rose on Inez Vaughan Hord on Mother's Day, ca. 1953.

3

Message in a Vase

My mother wasn't particularly interested in old or historical artifacts. I guess I took after my uncle, her brother, who always was the pack rat in the family. Even when he was 85 years old, he still kept almost everything. Mother preferred new, modern keepsakes.

In 1990, after Mother had died at age 79 and Dad has passed away five months later at age 84, my sister and I were preparing to sell the family home. We had been busy setting up everything for a weekend estate sale and had selected the items from the house that we wanted to keep. Our children, too, had made their selections.

Mother had kept very few of the normal keepsakes from her youth and had shared items from her mother with my sister and me through the years. A house fire many years ago had destroyed most of the family treasures to that point.

The night before the sale, I made one last sweep through the house to see if there was anything else that we needed to keep. I spied a small pewter bud vase sitting on a cabinet. I picked it up and turned it around in my hand several times. Then I decided I might use it sometime when my roses were blooming. I brought the vase, which is about six inches high, home with me and put it on my kitchen cabinet top.

After the sale ended, I was straightening my kitchen and decided to wash the vase and put it away. As I started to put it into the water, I noticed something in the narrow bottom of the vase. I got a pencil and fished out the small scrap of paper. There, in my

17

mother's handwriting, was a tiny note that read: "This vase was given to me by my grandmother Snavely when I was a little girl. There were two of them, but one was broken a long time ago."

I almost dropped the vase, I was so excited. I had nothing that had belonged to my great-grandmother—I thought. Then my mind went into motion, and I could vaguely remember seeing a vase like that before. I went through my cedar chest (it had been given to me by my grandparents when I was a little girl) and searched through my own personal keepsakes. Down in the bottom of the chest I found the matching vase. A large chip was broken out of its rim, but definitely it was the mate to the perfect one.

I treasure the vases, but most of all I treasure the note my mother had placed in the vase to be found after she was gone.

Fig. 6. The vases and the note found inside one.

4

On Father's Day

Today is Father's Day, a day we honor our fathers and recall favorite memories of our childhood with our dad. My dad has been gone for several years, but I have many fond memories of my childhood with him and his love for his wife and two daughters.

I remember how he sat through many piano recitals to hear his daughter, one of the last in line, perform her piano piece. He complained every time we had a recital, but he was right there on the front row when the time came, being the proud papa.

My daddy was a big tease. He loved to aggravate in a teasing way that made you love him more. When I was small, his grandmother, my great-grandmother, lived with his mother. We called her "Grandma." She was born in the mid-1800s and always wore a long dress with long sleeves and a chemise that she called a "shimmy." She also wore an apron at all times. He would rather tease Grandma than eat.

Daddy loved bacon and eggs and would eat them twice a day if Mother would let him. As he aged and did a lot of the cooking in the morning and at night, that's exactly what he ate. In addition, he loved working in the yard at their home at 931 West Crawford Street. He had flowers in the front and back yards and kept the grass groomed to perfection.

Homemade ice cream made in an old-fashioned hand-cranked mixer was a real treat for Daddy when we had company. Mother mixed the milk concoction, Daddy went to an ice house for a big block of ice, and with an ice pick he chipped big chunks to freeze the ice cream. The real work was in cranking the old machine, while keeping ice and salt packed around the ice cream can as it turned around and around. My sister was younger and smaller, so it became my duty to sit on the freezer to anchor it as Daddy cranked the lever. Towels protected my bottom, but what kept me there was the thought of a dish of his home-done ice cream. The only thing better was a dish of Ashburn's delicacy, a favorite of everyone in town.

Daddy gave me my first driving lessons, even though I took Driver's Education in high school and got my license then. One Saturday Daddy asked if I was ready for a driver's lesson. My sister Monna, who is six years my junior, and her puppy crawled in the back seat to go along for the excitement.

We took off going west on Crawford Street, and at first everything went okay. It had rained the day before, and Lillis Lane, which now runs north and south past McDaniel Junior High School, had not been paved and was a street full of ruts. Fortunately, in 1949 it saw little traffic. Aside from a few scary seconds when I got out of a rut and did a little sliding, the drive from Crawford Street to Morton went smoothly. Before Wal-Mart and all the other businesses grew up, Morton was just a low-traffic road coming in from Pottsboro. We turned east and headed back into town.

When we were on Morton, approaching Armstrong Avenue near Central Ward Elementary School, Daddy told me to slow down and turn right. In my excitement, I speeded up and tried to turn right. Wrong move. With Daddy and Monna yelling for me to stop and the puppy barking, I drove into the middle of Central's playground. I think that's when the decision was made that I should take Driver's Education. Louis Carlat took over and successfully taught me to drive.

Daddy was a Denison Yellow Jacket fan from way back, especially when his grandsons were playing. It didn't matter if it was basketball, football, or baseball, he was there if he had an opportunity to go.

He also loved to fish below the Denison Dam, but he rarely caught anything. It became a joke in the family whenever he gathered his fishing gear, put on his fishing hat and old clothes, and took off for the river. We waited for our fish dinner that rarely ever took place. He had fun, though, sitting quietly on the river bank and solving the problems of the world.

In my high school days, there was usually a midnight preview at the Rialto Theater, and Daddy was the designated driver. With a group of my girl friends, a trip to the Hive, Denison's youth center, usually ended with us walking to the Rialto for the late-night show. Daddy, bless him, would get up from his "nap" when I called for a ride home, come to town, "make the drag" on Main a couple of times, then deliver my friends safely to their homes.

Daddy was a caring person. My mother was the love of his life, and my sister and I were his pride and joy. I loved him dearly and will always remember him with special thoughts, especially on Father's Day.

Fig. 7. Monna Lue Hord and father, Lucious Hord, fishing, ca. 1947.

Fig. 8. Nancy Elizabeth "Lizzie" Duke Hawkins gets a bear hug from her grandson, Lucious R. Hord, in the early 1940s.

5

Grandma's Apron Strings

French maids once wore the cutest little white starched and ruffled aprons over their black uniforms. Aprons are almost a thing of the past today. Not so with our ancestors, who may have heard of Paris, Texas, but that's as close as they ever came to France.

Some aprons were similar to those cute ones worn by French maids, while others were more utilitarian and actually covered the front of a dress, including a bib. Most women today may own an apron or two, but find it hard to imagine wearing one all day long. We don't even want to stay in the kitchen long enough to get food on our clothing. Most of our aprons belonged to our mothers or grandmothers and today are collector's items.

Matters were very different for our grandmothers. Aprons were necessities, and no self-respecting mother or grandmother would be caught in the kitchen without one. Aprons were a practicality. They covered the owner's dress, keeping it clean longer and allowing it to be worn for four or five days or more. Having to hand-wash everything would certainly be an incentive to wear dresses more than one time.

My great-grandmother, Nancy Elizabeth "Lizzie" Duke Hawkins, also known as "Grandma," *always* wore an apron, even when she dressed up to go out. I'm surprised she took it off when she went to bed. Grandma was born in Tennessee in 1869 and died in 1949 in Denison.

Grandma made her aprons herself, usually to match and to cover her ankle-length dress. The bodice was kept clean by a bib that tied around her neck. Sometimes the apron had a smock-type top that protected even more of her dress. Her apron was tied with a string at her waist in back. She would wear the same one every day, except when she would take it off to launder it. In fact, her aprons would have holes in them before she threw them away and then usually because her mischievous grandson—my father, Lucious Robert Hord—would put his finger in the hole and rip the apron, forcing her to throw it away and get out a new one.

Daddy never outgrew his love for aggravating his grandmother. He always was a prankster, and he never passed Grandmother without untying her apron string. She would grab a broom or whatever was near her and chase him through the house. They both loved it, but at the time you would never have been able to convince Grandma that it was fun.

A friend, Don Barkley, has fond memories of his grandmother, who had four sons and grandsons, all of whom loved to tease her by untying her apron string. Don said they all learned to be quick when they pulled that string, because she always had a corsage pin stuck somewhere and "she was faster than Wild Bill Hickok and did not pull any punches if you were still within range." He soon learned to run if he was the guilty party, or even if he was just standing nearby. "Boy that thing could hurt," he remembered.

I had not thought of all the things I had seen Grandma use her apron for until a friend sent me an email titled "Apron." I had never even thought about an apron being so useful. I just may get some of mine out, although I'm not planning to stay in the kitchen any more than I already do.

It's pretty obvious that the principal use of Grandma's apron was to protect her dress underneath. But it also was just the right size to carry chips and kindling wood when she was starting the fire to cook that meal. It was perfect for wiping her perspiring brow when she was slaving over the old hot wood stove cooking the evening meal, and it served as a holder when she took her pans from the oven.

Aprons were great places for bashful children to hide behind when company came. They were good for drying the tears of a grandchild or great-grandchild, or for wiping a smear from a little one's mouth.

In Grandma's day, everyone who lived on a farm had chickens. The apron was great for carrying eggs into the house, or even eggs that were half-hatched and needed to be finished in a warming oven. Another friend of mine, Lavada Cuthbertson, said that having lived on a farm in her youth, she remembers gathering eggs out of the hen's nest and putting them in the apron to take in the house, all the while hoping that she didn't find a big chicken snake curled up in the hen's nest. It also made a good container to hold pecans that she gathered, she said.

When Grandma made a quick trip out into the yard on a cold day, an apron helped shield her from the cold when she wrapped it around her. It also held all sorts of vegetables brought in from the garden. After the peas had been shelled, it was a good way to carry out the hulls. In the fall, it might be used to bring in the apples that had fallen off the tree.

Gerry Daugherty remembers her grandmothers Chick and McDonald wearing aprons as part of their everyday clothes. Gerry said many times she helped fill their aprons with eggs, veggies, and other things for which extra hands were needed. She also has an apron that belonged to a dear friend, Aubrey Sampson, who gave it to her just before she left to live with a son in Houston. Aubrey was a wonderful cook.

I never thought of it before, but the apron was handy when Grandma saw company driving up into the yard. She could make a quick spin around the room and dust the furniture. It probably worked just as well as those newfangled dusting contraptions we have today.

When she had dinner ready, Grandma could walk out onto the porch and wave her apron so that the men who were working out in the fields—or maybe out back with the Model T—would know that it was time to come inside to wash up and eat.

Can you think of anything today that has so many uses? It may be a long time before someone invents something to replace that old-fashioned apron.

But Grandma wasn't the only one to benefit from aprons. They reach all the way back to Adam and Eve, who connected fig leaves to form an apron of sorts for a different purpose—to hide their nakedness.

Some aprons protect workers from dirty, laborious and dangerous work. Butchers, waiters, carpenters, and welders use them today, and they are specially designed for their occupations. Leather aprons protected blacksmiths and welders, keeping the sparks of fire from burning their clothing. Aprons were used as a means of distinguishing different jobs—maybe for a gardener, spinner, weaver, garbage handler, butler, barber, stonemason, and others.

Restaurant workers still wear simple canvas aprons that will hold their ticket books, pens and possibly their tips.

No matter what type apron a person wears today, it is still a protection for something or a darn good emergency basket. We all should have at least one apron.

Fig. 9. Nancy Elizabeth "Lizzie" Duke Hawkins.

6

Tennessee Roots

In the last chapter, we discussed my great-grandmother, Nancy Elizabeth "Lizzie" Duke Hawkins ("Grandma") and her aprons. As time passed, I became deeply involved in genealogy and gathering notes about our family tree. Along the way, I discovered that Grandma was one of fourteen children born to John Adam Duke and Nancy Elizabeth Parker. The family lived at Manchester, Tennessee, a little town about sixty miles southeast of Nashville. Evidently Grandma was the only sibling to migrate to Texas. The remainder stayed in the Manchester area and continued to be a pretty close-knit group.

Grandma and a sister, Mary Lucy Duke Bush, corresponded until their deaths, then others in the family kept in contact with two of Mary Bush's daughters, Delia and Connie. My dad had stayed in touch with these two maiden cousins, far advanced in years, and I wanted to do the same.

My husband and I made our first trip to Tennessee in 1978 and met the Bush family, including the two elderly sisters, who I believed could answer some of my questions about Grandma's family members.

The sisters took us to the Gilley Hill Cemetery—one of the most peaceful spots you can imagine, sitting atop a hill surrounded by trees, with a small Methodist church nearby. Resting there are family burial plots dating back to Grandma's grandparents, Gideon Floid Duke and Elizabeth King, or even to the Revolutionary War.

The Bush sisters have kept the graves there their whole lives, and I do mean "kept." They carried the dirt to the cemetery in tubs in the back of their car, to keep the mounds on each family grave—including that of one of Grandma's children who died before she came to Texas. There isn't a blade of grass to be found on any of the graves, because "Grandpa said there should be no grass growing on his family's graves," one said; and they carry dirt to the cemetery "because mama and pap told us to."

The last weekend each May is Decoration Day in Tennessee, and that's just what people with loved ones in Gilley Hill Cemetery do—they decorate. For days before the last Sunday in that month, they clean the cemetery and place flowers on the graves. Then, on Sunday, they have church services, dinner on the grounds, and singing in the afternoon.

It's a time when family and friends get together, sometimes the only time they see one another all year, for some good old-fashioned visiting. It's a good custom, and the fellowship between these relatives and friends is evidence of why the custom has continued for so many years. They look forward to the day.

It sometimes seems to me that there must be more Dukes in Tennessee than almost any other family group. Back in 1987, at a Duke family reunion in Manchester, we met more than 130 of them. That reunion was planned by a "cousin" from another branch of the family, Jewell Christian, with the help of one from still another branch—Lyndol Duke. Jewell's mother, who is nearing 90, was the oldest person present.

Some of the Tennessee relatives remembered Grandma going back for only one visit after moving to Texas. At that time, she told them that Texas was her home now, and if they wanted to see her again, they could come to Texas to do it. She kept her word, too, but none came to Texas until after her death. By the time they got here, there were no Hawkins in the telephone book who were related to her, and they couldn't locate any of the Denison relatives.

As frequently happens, we drove more than 600 miles to the reunion, only to find a couple of cousins who live near me in Texas—one in Plano and another in Fort Worth. Both were present, and it was exciting to find distant relatives living so close to our home.

Searching for your "roots" can be as time-consuming as you want to make it. It takes great patience to search out family information for generations back, so it's great when you find someone who has done much of that work for you.

Such is the case with Don Duke, a visiting professor at East Carolina University. He has been gathering information on the Duke family tree for many years and provided those attending the reunion with interesting details. In fact, Don went a little above and beyond, tracing the family all the way back to Japeth, third son of Noah, and then to the Biblical Adam.

One of the most interesting ancestors was William Duke, who was accused of being responsible for the first shots fired in Bacon's Rebellion, the forerunner of the Revolutionary War. This may or may not qualify me for membership in the Daughters of the American Revolution. We'll have to see.

Finding even a few of your distant relatives can be a very rewarding experience. After the 1987 reunion, it took me a while to absorb my family's connections with all those people and to figure out who belonged to which branch of the Duke family tree.

Around 1992, my husband and I went back to Manchester to visit the Bush sisters again. When we arrived at their house, their brother Lemuel, who was on crutches, was waiting with them. After all the pleasantries were out of the way, they asked if we were ready to go the cemetery.

So, camera in hand, we drove them out to the cemetery. We walked along the path, between many graves on which there was no grass growing, only mounds of dirt. Each grave was decorated with flowers by the elderly ladies.

They pointed out each family site, saying, "Here's where Aunt Rose is buried; here's where Grandpa is buried; here's where Lemuel's leg is buried; here's where Mama is buried."

I stopped them and said, "Back up a minute, who did you say was buried back here?" They replied that Lemuel had a problem with his leg—I think diabetes—and it was amputated and buried in his plot. When he came to die, he would be buried with it.

When we came back home, I was telling an elderly friend about the experience, and she asked, "Is that what you call having one foot in the grave?"

Lemuel died not long after our visit. I think of this story every time I recall the two little ladies who became my great friends. We were back in Tennessee in April 2003, and the oldest one had just passed away and gone to Gilley Hill, leaving the 92-year-old alone.

Fig. 10. Exploring the Gilley Hill Cemetery.

7

R.C. Vaughan, My "Unkie"

My uncle used to tell people he was the only uncle I ever had. I've always told people he was my favorite uncle. Both statements were true.

Age caught up with the man I called "Unkie" until I got so old he told me to call him "R.C.," because "Unkie" made him feel old. However, he's still "Unkie" to my sister Monna's and my children, our grandchildren, and my great-grandchildren.

Tuesday morning I lost my uncle, but I'm sure he is in a better place. After all, we had him for more than ninety-four years. He had a great life and did things just about as he wanted to do them.

Most people called my uncle Judge Vaughan, and he was just that. A colleague and good friend, Judge Lloyd Perkins, said that he was known throughout the state as a "judge's judge." We have always had a mutual admiration society all our own.

From the time he returned to Denison after graduating from the University of Texas Law School until my sister Monna was born in 1941, my mother's brother doted on his only niece. After that, Monna and I shared his admiration.

As someone who was involved in almost everything going on in Grayson County, he lectured me about learning to say "no" and not getting so involved. I tried, but I'm afraid that, like him, I had trouble turning people down.

My grandparents had several children, but only R.C. and my mother grew to adulthood. I have several stories that I've always liked to tell on my uncle, and whenever I would begin speaking at a

31

meeting we both were attending, he knew almost for certain one story that I would tell, and a grin would pass over his face.

When he and his parents and sister moved back to Denison from Hollis, Oklahoma, my mother was already in school at Golden Rule Elementary. While R.C. started school when he was four or five years old, he hadn't yet learned to read. My grandmother, Anna Vaughan, had a large garden a few yards behind their house on Coffin Street in Denison's Cotton Mill community.

R.C. and my mother, like most siblings, did a lot of arguing. One day their mother went to work in the garden after lunch, and she told them to take care of the dishes. The argument began, and R.C. refused to help. He probably was four years old. Mother finally said, "If you won't help me, will you take a note to Momma in the garden?" That sounded great to him, so he carried the note down to his mother, who read it and said, "R.C., go back in the house and help Inez do the dishes." I think that may be part of the reason he studied so hard and was able to enter the University of Texas when he was only fifteen years old.

While the family was living in Oklahoma, my grandfather, Ben Vaughan, bought a Model "T" Ford when R.C. was just a baby. My grandmother drove it around town. One day she was driving on a country road with my mother sitting in the rumble seat, holding baby R.C. Mama was trying to miss all the bumps and dips in the road. Unfortunately, she hit a big one, and R.C. bounced out of my mother's arms and out of the car and landed in the road.

My mother yelled, but it took my grandmother a while to stop the car. A man and woman in a horse-drawn wagon saw the child sail out of the car and stopped and picked him up and took him to his mother. I don't think my mother ever was trusted to hold him again, and he rode in the front seat thereafter. Later, when someone tried to heckle him, he told this true story, ending by saying, "That's my excuse, what's yours?"

R.C. always admitted that he was a "mama's boy." His mother was determined that he was going to get a good education, and he has always given her credit for his graduating from law school. He paid most of his own expenses at UT by working as a waiter and dishwasher in a boarding house. It was a plus that he played in the

Longhorn Band. His mother was truly proud of his accomplishments.

When he came back to Denison after graduating and opened an office in the old Security Building, his salary as assistant city attorney was $50 a month, a sum that paid all his office expenses while he began to build a small office practice. Once he was promoted to city attorney of Denison, his salary went up to $150 a month. On both salaries, he always jokingly said, he nearly starved to death.

R.C. was always a historian. As a child I remember him placing his reel-to-reel tape recorder in out-of-the-way places during family dinners or table games. He said that he was recording history. We didn't think much about it until we had children of our own and he came out with that recorder and played back some of those recordings at family gatherings.

I remember in particular one time when my sister Monna's young daughters, Bebe and Melinda Buckley, were present. He played a recording of their mother saying her nursery rhymes and the two of us singing Christmas carols. Those little girls rolled on the floor laughing at our young voices. He put those reel-to-reel recordings on cassette tapes, and it's fun now to listen to some of the conversations when no one knew they were being recorded.

Later R.C. got a fairly large recording machine and interviewed many of the old-timers around Denison and Sherman, telling stories you wouldn't believe about the area. Now, it is wonderful to listen to those recordings and hear the voices of some of the people he knew and admired.

Many people don't know that R.C. had a wonderful voice and often sang solos at Calvary Baptist in Denison, where he grew up. Even in later years, he would sing as he and his son Charles drove around Grayson County remembering its history. At the drop of a hat, he would come out with a rousing rendition of "The Eyes of Texas," a tune he never forgot and one that his family and friends sang at his graveside service on Saturday.

One year he took his two sons, Jim and Charles, and my two sons, Rob and Brian, on a trip to Colorado. The boys had a wonderful time, but R.C. decided against ever doing it again. Four young boys were a handful.

Many years ago, R.C. and I took his mother (my grandmother, Anna Vaughan) on another trip—her first commercial airline flight. She was ninety-two years old and, as always, an adventurer at heart. The flight was from Dallas–Fort Worth Regional Airport to Houston International Airport.

A fast trip it was, too. Because of traffic problems at DFW, the plane took off thirty minutes late. The pilot promised to try to make up some time once he was airborne. Twenty-five minutes later, he announced that he was approaching the Houston airport. Momma Vaughan was only half-finished with her soft drink and peanuts, provided by the airline, when hostesses began collecting glasses. Whirlwind trips through the airports in Dallas and Houston were no problem for Momma, who rode comfortably in wheelchairs provided by Braniff.

More than forty-five years earlier, she had taken her first airplane ride at the old Gray Field, located east of Denison. She was the only member of her family brave enough to climb into the small two-seater plane for a casual ride above the treetops of Denison and Sherman. She said the ride cost five dollars, considerably less than today's rates, and the pilot was a very smooth driver and pulled no "funny business." Through the years she had always said she would like to take a flight to the moon, but she never really expected to go aloft.

About 28 years earlier, a three-year-old youngster named Richard Albert Penn Jr. came to live with her when his father purchased the old Loi-Mac Pharmacy. This youngster played a big part in her life until he was in junior high school and his father died. He then went to military school in San Marcos. Momma and "Penn" remained close through the years, and he was about to be married to Sandra Leake in a chapel ceremony at the First Baptist Church in Houston. Momma was anxious to attend.

Fearing that a long trip by car would be too tiring for her, R.C. and I decided to fly with her to the wedding. Joining us on the whirlwind flight to Houston were two other grandchildren— Jim Vaughan of Sherman and my sister Monna Hord Buckley of Allen—and a great-granddaughter, Mindy Buckley. While Dramamine, chewing gum, and other "crutches" were used by the more seasoned passengers, Momma wasn't even nervous as the plane soared above the clouds, which to her looked like "the most beautiful snow I've ever seen."

Upon her return home, she pronounced her voyage a "way out and way up weekend." Topping it off, she stopped by Wilson N. Jones Hospital in Sherman for a first visit with her first great-great-granddaughter, Donna Nicole Hunt, born June 11, 1981, to Mr. and Mrs. Brian Hunt. All in all, it was a weekend Momma said she would never forget.

During his mother's last years, before she passed away at 96, R.C. spent weekends with her at her home in Denison. During that time they did a lot of talking, and he did a lot of interviewing and wrote a lot of notes about stories she told him. Later he wrote about her in some of his newspaper columns, and we published a small book on her life, complete with family pictures.

As his cousin, Dick Hefton of Oklahoma City, said on Tuesday morning after being told that R.C. had passed away, "For so many years I thought of R.C. as a son of the community and a property of the State of Texas. This really marks the end of an historical era." It does indeed.

Fig. 11. Judge R.C. Vaughan.

Fig. 12. Donna Hord holding sister Monna Lue, ca. 1942.

8

Piano Lessons

The name Bebe Bodamer has cropped up several times lately, and I hadn't thought about my piano teacher from eons ago for a long time until now.

Mrs. Bodamer. I never really knew if Bebe was a Miss or if she had ever been married, but a look in a 1949 Denison City Directory found her listed as the widow of Daniel Bodamer.

At a very young age, I began taking piano lessons from Lula Mae Hays at 815 West Gandy Street. I learned to play a lot of scales, and I'm sure I was taught the basics for a seven-year-old, but I wanted to play popular tunes and songs I had heard before. So sometime in my early years of elementary school, my parents signed me up with Bebe Bodamer. Her studio was in her home at 218 West Gandy, just down the street from the public library.

I took one lesson a week and was supposed to practice an hour each day between visits. Therein lay the problem. I didn't like to practice. We had an old player piano—one that could do its own thing when music rolls were inserted. It was much more fun to listen to the music playing automatically than to make my own.

Mother was determined that I was going to be a concert pianist. Now that's a laugh. She would sit with me on the piano stool and tap out the beat with a fly swatter. The fly swatter had a dual function, because Mother had been known to do a little swatting with it when things didn't go right. Today, she possibly

37

could have been cited for child abuse if someone heard my yelling and her swatting.

I probably deserved every swat, and it did me no harm. Sometimes I think a few good swats might do some of the unruly kids today a little good. But back to Bebe Bodamer.

Tommy Loy, whom I ran into when he was playing trumpet at the Sacramento Jazz Festival, also was a student of Bebe. My long-time friend, Patsy Christman Hampton of Reno, Nevada, was at the festival with us. She too took piano lessons from Mrs. Bodamer. All three of us remembered Bebe as a feisty little lady who stood beside the piano and tapped out the beat with a pointer stick. I was never certain that she wasn't going to whack me if I hit a wrong key and was usually a little nervous during lessons. She could always tell if I hadn't practiced. I wonder how. Tommy said he had been thinking about her and all the patience she had with us.

We had a yearly recital, and we worked on our numbers for months. Usually we remembered and did well, but occasionally we froze. I'll never forget my dad's fake pleasure in attending those recitals. As I got older, I played nearer the end, and he had to sit through the whole thing. He was usually fit to be tied.

Another friend, Elayne Tignor Vick, grew up in Denison and is several years younger than I. Elayne said that for what seemed like years, her mother took her to the Bodamer Studio for piano lessons. Elayne was willing to go, so long as she didn't have to play in any of the recitals. She remembered Bebe as a "funny old lady."

I'll have to give Mrs. B. her due, though. She was a talented woman who seems to have played just about every instrument. Patsy recalls taking lessons from her upstairs at 427 West Main Street. I guess she moved to Gandy during that period and that Patsy started taking lessons before I did.

I learned what a small world we live in when I mentioned taking lessons from Mrs. B. while talking to my uncle, Judge R.C. Vaughan. Lo and behold, he said he, too, took lessons from her when he was in high school. I knew that he had played the bass clarinet in the Denison High School Band and went on to the University of Texas and played in the Texas Longhorn Band, but I had never known that he took lessons from "my" teacher.

38

He told me that my mother also took piano lessons from her. I guess she had mentioned it before, but I had forgotten. I came by not wanting to practice honestly, because he said Mother and her mom would go round and round when practice time came. My grandmother gave up on mother, though, and she didn't take lessons very long. That could be the reason my mother was so determined that I would learn to play.

R.C. even played in Mrs. Bodamer's Little Symphony Orchestra, which was made up of her students. During the time he was taking lessons, he remembered, she taught from a two-story house east of the Traveler's Hotel. He said that, until now, few people had known that he played in a symphony orchestra.

Mrs. B. played the oboe with the young musicians and also played with the Dallas Symphony Orchestra. My uncle recalled that she would ride the Interurban to Dallas for orchestra practice and performances, catching her ride in front of the Katy Depot.

Another friend, Paul Jennings, remembered taking lessons from Mrs. Bodamer, too. Paul played the trumpet for many, many functions around Denison for years and now is a retired school administrator. He was Bebe's student between 1943 and 1951, and he remembers playing in her band when students gathered every Saturday morning upstairs in that building on West Main. The group sometimes played concerts in the educational building of the "old" Waples Methodist Church.

Included among those student musicians—who all took their own music stands with them to practice—were Otis Williams, Joe Wilson, Nancy Stroud, Gilbert Brigham, Phillip Noe, Tommy Loy, and Jennings. Tommy Loy's lesson with Mrs. B. was scheduled just before Paul's. Nancy Stroud and a girl named Gill, from Pottsboro, accompanied them on the piano. Paul recalls that Nancy was a very talented pianist who went on to play piano professionally in Dallas. Nancy and I played mud-pies together before we entered first grade, but that's as far as the resemblance went.

Former students sometimes would come back and play with the Saturday band, Paul recalled. Paul remembered one in particular, violinist Bobby Pipkin, as a very good musician. Tommy Little and Pat Corcoran played the accordion, he recalled.

Paul mentioned one point about Mrs. B. that I had forgotten: she always played and taught with white gloves on. "The gloves were good for a few clinkers when she played, but after all, she was the teacher and no one ever said anything," he claimed. He said she was related to the Charles Bohnefeld Cleaners family.

As noted above, Bebe moved to the 200 block of West Gandy, and that's where I began taking piano lessons. I'm now sorry to say that my mother's determination was pretty much in vain. I played some in younger years and possibly could pick it up again if I worked at it, but I was never what might be considered a "good" pianist. I've always envied those people who could "play by ear" and just sit down and play what they want to. I guess it's a natural talent that I just don't have.

Bebe Bodamer was a neat lady, and I'm sure that she left her mark on many would-be musicians. Thank goodness that a few actually accomplished something as a result of her efforts.

Fig. 13. A young R.C. Vaughan with his father, Grayson County Commissioner S.B. "Ben" Vaughan.

40

9

Spanish Club Trip

Anyone who has ever graduated from high school anywhere no doubt has memories of class activities or maybe a trip out of town taken with a group of classmates.

Elayne Tignor Vick, Denison High School Class of 1958, wrote an article for a 2003 class reunion that brought back memories for me. Elayne now lives in Irving, Texas, with her husband, Dossie, a member of my Class of 1953. Elayne is a writer and editor for Sabre Holdings at Southlake.

The title of Elayne's piece was "Veni, Vidi, Vici," which she said is all she remembers from her Latin class at DHS. It means "We Came, We Saw, We Conquered." Elayne recalled a bus trip to Galveston with her fellow Latin students to attend a Junior Classical League convention. Miss Edith Austin and Miss Mildred Walker, teachers, were the chaperones who were brave enough to accept the challenge of keeping up with the group.

This reminded me of a similar Spanish Club trip in 1952 or 1953 with Miss Walker, our Spanish teacher, and a few parents as chaperones. We rode a school bus to Austin to attend the annual conference of the Pan American Student Forum of Texas (PASF), if my memory hasn't failed me.

Riding a school bus on a trip is nothing like taking off on a Greyhound or Continental bus. We knew not to expect any comfort or conveniences, but the togetherness of the students made up for anything we would find missing today.

Austin was much smaller then, and there were no freeways. We followed Highway 75 all the way, and once we got into Austin, we rode on a regular two-way street. It was paved, though—it wasn't *that* long ago.

Actually, we made two trips to Central Texas. The second was to San Antonio, where we visited the Alamo and all the Spanish missions, to learn a little history at first hand. In Austin, we went to the Texas State Capitol and the University of Texas campus.

I don't remember much about what transpired during the conference, but I do remember that our contribution to the program was the "Mexican Hat Dance," in which a group of us danced in costume. I can still hear the peppy music that made our feet heel-and-toe and shuffle around the huge hat in the center.

What I remember most is what happened when we started home. Before we passed Austin's city limits, we stopped for a lunch break at a spot with a couple of restaurants in sight. Miss Walker told us to be back on the bus in one hour. As we got off the bus, a UT student told Bettye Hendrix (now Hauser), Patti Duggan (now Davey), and me that a better place to eat was just around the corner, so off we trekked.

It was a very nice place to get a hamburger, but the service was anything but fast. We waited, waited, and waited before we finally got our food. We probably lost all consciousness of time and, when we finished eating, we strolled back to the bus. To our surprise, the bus was gone. Here we were, three teenage girls left in the middle of Austin with nowhere to go.

It happened that I knew a Denison boy—I cannot remember his name—who was attending the University of Texas. I just happened to have his telephone number, because we had talked while our group was in Austin. I gave him a call and told him of our plight. He didn't have a car, but he could borrow one from a friend and said he would come pick us up and take us to chase the bus. He arrived in a flash, in an old jalopy convertible that didn't even have a front window. But we piled in and headed north.

After traveling a few blocks, we saw a big yellow bus heading south toward us. We began to wave our arms and yell, but the bus went right on by us just like we weren't there. My friend turned around and followed the bus back to the restaurants, where it finally stopped.

The three of us thanked him and very quietly headed to the open door on our bus. Miss Walker was sitting near the front of the bus, and we had to pass her to find seats near the back. Not a word was uttered, but if looks could kill, we would have been dead. After that, everyone was counted before the bus pulled out. She never mentioned the incident. I guess she was relieved that she found us.

On one of the trips, we stayed in a motel with four to a room. There was a lot of prowling around from room to room the first night, and that brought a stern lecture. The second night, about ten or more of us got together in one room and spent the entire night talking and sleeping crossways on the bed.

As we got on the bus the next morning, Miss Walker came to the back of the bus, where we always liked to sit, and thanked us for staying in our rooms and being so quiet. Little did she know that half the rooms were empty all night long.

As Elayne said, "Everyone got home safely, but the tales told around school afterward were of a wild time." Ditto for the classes a few years earlier. We didn't speak Latin, and very few of us learned to speak Spanish. I certainly don't know the Spanish translation for the Latin "Veni, Vidi, Vici," but this merely goes to prove that just about any class can say, "We Came, We Saw, We Conquered."

Fig. 14. Spanish Club members at fish pond, during visit to Alamo, San Antonio.

Fig. 15. Donna Hord, ca. 1953. Background: The Denison Herald's *1956 full-page feature about high school youth center, the Hive.*

10

Remembering the Hive

During the 1950s, some time before, and some time after, Denison's young people had a secure, supervised place to go at night where they could meet friends and have a good time.

I guess things were a little different in the 1950s. All kids didn't have cars, and parents set strictly enforced curfews. But kids still wanted to get together in the evening for a little dancing, games, or plain old being with each other to talk and laugh.

In Denison, that place was called "The Hive." It was upstairs at 309-1/2 West Woodard Street. Once you climbed the steep stairway, you entered a world established especially for teenagers.

Tuesday nights were just for "hanging out," with the youth center open from 7 until 9 P.M. Then, on Friday and Saturday nights, the doors were open a little longer. Only students and their guests were admitted, and each had to register upon arrival.

At one time Mrs. Stella Hollingsworth (later Morrison) was in charge, and she ran a strict but friendly ship. Everyone loved Mrs. Hollingsworth.

I hadn't thought about the Hive for a long time until last week, when I had a phone call from Bob Onstot of Denison, who was trying to locate an old buddy of his. He and Harvey Patrick Malone both graduated from Denison High School in 1954.

Bob said that Pat had contacted him a while back, looking for information on the Hive. He couldn't find what he remembered he had kept, but recently he ran across it—a full-page feature in *The*

Denison Herald of October 14, 1956. He tried to contact Pat where he had been living, in Cedar City, Tennessee, but could not find him. He said that he, Pat, and Arthur Melson had been buddies in high school. Arthur passed away recently.

Bob, who himself has been in ill health in recent years, retired as a satellite engineer on one of the teams that installed the first Mercury Satellite Systems for NASA.

The feature page told about an open house planned at the Hive as a "typical Hive activities" night, according to Rev. David Jones, chairman of the board of directors, so that parents could see the youth center program in action. The only change from the youth center routine was the serving of refreshments. On a regular night the snack bar was open, but teens had to purchase their snacks.

At that time, the teenagers had been helping to spruce up the center by doing some of the work themselves. A series of murals made up of caricatures of popular musicians and singers had been painted on the east wall of the Hive ballroom. The paintings were a group effort by Mike Malone, Sonny Miller, and Bobby Onstot. This was where the jukebox was located. If someone had a quarter (or maybe less; I don't remember what it cost to play a record), the teens could dance if they had a dance partner.

Other wall decorations were scattered strategically around the large center. The students had painted the ballroom, snack bar, and lounge room, as well as the murals. They had sanded and varnished the dance floor—a task that, according to the article, required a lot of elbow grease.

To buy materials for the job, a special fund had been accumulated from half the jukebox receipts that the Hive received. The modern jukebox was a pay-as-you-dance music box. It held 100 records; some new ones, mostly popular dance numbers and standards, had been installed to help assure the success of the open house.

Adult supervision at the Hive in 1956 was supplied by Gene Eubank, assisted by members of the Denison Service League, who took turns helping out there, usually operating the snack bar. Eubank later became Denison's police chief for a number of years until he retired. Members of the Parent-Teachers Association also helped staff the youth center.

During the four years that I was a student at Denison High School, the Hive was a destination at least once a week and sometimes more often. Saturday nights, with or without a date, meant at least a stop at the Hive to see who was there and what was going on.

From the Hive, some girl friends and I frequently went to the midnight preview at the Rialto Theater. If I didn't have a date, my dad always received a call about 1 A.M. to pick us up and take us home. He was so good to drag Main Street after he picked us up, then silently take my friends home before we headed home ourselves.

If I remember correctly, junior-senior proms in 1952 and 1953 were at the Hive. I remember a lot of elaborate decorating taking place before each one. Those stairs weren't easy to conquer in formal prom dresses and high heels, but at that age we didn't worry about it.

Times have changed. Those of us who remember the Hive have fond memories, but it is doubtful that such a youth center would be at the top of the entertainment list for teenagers today. The Hive is no longer operating, and there are no midnight previews or even movies at the Rialto Theater. Still, teens today somehow seem to find their own entertainment—hopefully clean, safe, and wholesome.

Fig. 16. Denison High School Student Council, ca. 1953.

*Fig. 17. Lucious Hord (left) and a friend on Main Street in Denison,
1934.*

11

Drug Store Days

Growing up in a drug store in the 1950s was like growing up in world completely different from the world of today. I don't mean a super drug store like so many we have today. The 1950 variety now would be called "mom and pop" stores. But the extras they provided are still longed for by those who experienced them.

My dad owned and operated Loi-Mac Pharmacy at 200 West Main Street for a number of years. Our drug store had a magazine rack with lots of comic books, movie magazines, and other reading material. It had a post office, pharmacy, over-the-counter medicine racks, a cashier's cage, a cigar case, cosmetics, toiletries, a gift area, and a soda fountain. The fountain had real ice-cream tables and chairs, a grill, a malt and milk shake mixer, and real hometown (Ashburn's) ice cream.

There was even a beauty shop upstairs on the balcony, where Alma Baker and Katherine Cox styled hair for the women of Denison. First the beauty shop was in the front of the building, and later it moved to the back of the store. In both places, inside stairways led to the shop. I remember the old-fashioned permanent machines that looked like something from outer space and were used before "cold waves" became popular. I remember sitting on a box to have my hair curled by one of those contraptions. Sometimes the smell of the permanent-wave solution got pretty strong, but women, then as now, would go through a lot to be gorgeous.

Dad and a partner purchased Loi-Mac Drug Store in 1946. As soon as I was old enough, I think when I was about fourteen years old, I began helping out. At first I manned the cash register, but as my experience grew, so did my duties. For the next two or three years, I stocked the shelves, waited on customers, took orders over the phone (we had a delivery service), took payments on charge accounts, manned the post office, and even swept out when needed. I may have washed dishes at the soda fountain a few times when we were really busy, but, like most teenagers, I didn't relish washing dishes.

This was in the day when Hadacol was all the rage for what ailed everyone. It was amazing how fast that Hadacol disappeared from the shelf. Ladies' nylon hose with seams up the back also were popular—when we could get them.

Christmas, Valentine's Day, and Mother's Day were special times. We sold a lot of candy and other gifts, and almost everyone wanted them gift-wrapped. We all did the wrapping, Barney Kepler included, and we didn't charge extra for that service. A lot of our customers were seniors who couldn't get out and come to the store, so our delivery business was brisk. We all took orders, and Barney delivered them as quickly as he could.

I remember our giant cash register with all the numbers and a crank on the side to open it. I remember our charge ticket case, where Daddy kept up with who owed him what. Recently I saw an almost identical one at an antique mall on Main Street; the price was staggering.

Charge tickets were written in pencil, with the carbon copy given to the customer and the original filed under the customer's name on a large metal slab with springs to hold them secure. At the end of the month, the bookkeeper would take all the tickets under that person's slot and send a bill. It was a simple operation, and we had not heard of computers. All posting was done by hand, and all records were handwritten into books. I wonder what happened to all those books.

Don't ask me why, but I never worked at the soda fountain. I like to think I was the official taster. I loved the sounds of the milkshakes and malts being mixed, the sizzle of the grill, and the creativity of the banana splits and sundaes. Best of all, I loved the regular customers who depended on us for their coffee breaks and quick lunches. Many of those customers are still my friends.

Being somewhat of a collector, the thing I regret most is those ice cream tables and chairs. There were about six sets down the east side of the drug store, where people could have lunch. They were the ideal place to do homework on the nights when I worked. These were the "real thing," with chrome bands on the table and black wrought-iron chairs. As I remember, Daddy got tired of those "uncomfortable" things and took them to the trash dump. He brought in newer, more comfortable, more modern red plastic-covered booths that took up twice the space. I'll never get over that move. Whenever I go into an antique store and see a set, I always look at the price tag and cry.

Our drug store was just across the street from Curley O'Donnell's Roll-r-Bowl at 131 West Main. It was heavily patronized by airmen from Perrin Air Force Base. For refreshments, many visited our soda fountain. I met a lot of nice—and some not so nice—airmen, but only dated one of them briefly. It was fun talking to them, though, when they stopped by for a soda or a Coke.

Downstairs at Curley's were the bowling lanes, and upstairs was the skating rink. Saturday mornings were reserved for students to skate. My group of friends religiously went skating. I've never been particularly well balanced on my feet; put me on roller skates, and I'm headed for a fall. I did a lot of *trying* to skate but never got the hang of it. Sometimes the skating rink was turned into a boxing ring, where many young Denison men showed what they could do.

During those days, we had plenty of drug stores in Denison. In addition to Loi-Mac, there was Harris Drug at 221 West Main Street, and Lone Star Drug in the 100 block of Main.

Let's not forget Bear Drug at 230 West Main, on the corner across from both the State National and Citizens National banks. At Bear Drug, Lee Anderson operated a soda fountain that people still remember for its hamburgers and milkshakes. Upstairs above Bear Drug were the offices of many of Denison's physicians and dentists.

My dad once worked at Kingston Drug as a "soda jerk" (I'm not being disrespectful here; that's what they called a person who "jerked" sodas). Kingston's is where my mother met my dad many years earlier, when he was working at the soda fountain, and she worked there herself in the 1950s. Out front, Kingston's had a big thermometer where everyone checked to see how hot or cold it was, 24 hours a day. The store's motto was "Kingston's Has It," and it prominently advertised its affiliation with "Rexall" drugs. According to Wikipedia, between 1920 and 1977, as many as 12,000 drug stores across the United States were licensed to use the Rexall brand. (The "Rex" in the name came from the common Rx abbreviation for drug prescriptions.)

I worked at Burtis Drug at 408 West Main, before going off to college.

A friend, Thelma Hastings Harris, also spent a lot of time in a drug store, some of it behind the soda fountain. Her father, J.F. Landers, operated a clothing store next door. Both buildings were later torn down to accommodate a new and larger Citizens National Bank, later Chase Bank.

Thelma and her husband, Robert Harris, purchased their drug store in 1944. Robert had worked at Bear Drug before going into business for himself. Bear Drug's owner, Charles Sherrard, had opened a second Bear Drug branch in the 221 West Main location but was willing to sell it to the Harrises. The couple operated their drug store for twelve years.

Thelma remembered Mabel Dancy, who cooked the best hamburgers she ever ate. Thelma was no slouch in making pies, especially lemon, and she baked them to sell in the store. Engineers working on the Denison Dam had offices on the building's second floor. Thelma recalled that they were very good customers and ate lots of lemon pies.

According to Thelma, there was a hotel on the third floor of their building and the Landers building next door, with a stairway between the two businesses. She couldn't remember the name of the hotel, and neither can I.

In 1956, the Harrises sold the store, and it was demolished to build the new bank. As a young woman, Thelma had wanted to be a schoolteacher, but she was fifty years old when she went back to school and earned her degree. She taught a couple of years at Central Ward School, then in Lubbock. She retired after thirteen years on the job at Arlington and passed away on May 18, 2003.

Recently my sister, Monna Buckley of McKinney, called and said she was coming up for lunch. I started thinking about where I would take her to eat. Since both of us have gotten into researching our family history and collecting photographs, we took a nostalgic trip to Barrett Drug's soda fountain.

Barrett's has the closest thing I've found to our dad's fountain. The main differences are that we had a grill and they don't, and I don't see banana splits any more. We sat at an ice- cream table and had sandwiches, chips, and Cokes.

We reminisced about the "good old days," although Monna is younger. I thought she didn't remember as much about the Loi-Mac as I did. Well, I was wrong. She remembered Roy Rogers coming into the store; I didn't. When Roy visited, the deliveryman, Barney Kepler, was standing close to the cash register and took his money. The rest of the employees were all excited, but Barney didn't realize who Roy was.

Occasionally I see a photo of our old Loi-Mac Drug Store. My friend Billy Holcomb has brought me a couple, and I have a couple of pictures of an Eisenhower parade that were taken from across the street, showing the store front as it was then.

A few years ago, I ran across a clipping showing scenes from early Denison. One was headed "Ye Olde Time Drug Store of the Days of 1908." The stools at the soda fountain rang a bell in my head. Then it dawned on me that the stools and the ice-cream tables and chairs were the ones that had been at Loi-Mac Drug. Sure enough, information under the picture read, "This was one swanky drug and soda water emporium back in the 1890s." The picture was taken by a photographer with a big camera and a black hood in which he hid himself during the operation, the caption said. The picture was of the old Hanna Drug Store, established in 1873 at 210 West Main. It was later taken over by W.J. Furman and R.E. McCormick and moved to 200 West Main.

On Mr. Furman's death, his wife and her son Jimmy operated the store. Then they sold it to McCormick and Lois Wallace, later Richardson, who named it Loi-Mac Drug. The store's name combined "Mac" and "Loi" after both of them. McCormick and Lois operated Loi-Mac until my dad, Lucious R. Hord, and Roscoe Pace bought it in 1946. Both men had previously been connected with Kingston's Drug, although Daddy had been in the insurance business for ten years.

In 1952, the store was sold to R.A. Penn, who operated it until his death, when the business closed.

Fig. 18. Lucious R. Hord in his drugstore, Loi-Mac Pharmacy.

12

A Visit With Lady Bird Johnson

A barbecue on the banks of the Pedernales River at the LBJ Ranch is not greatly unlike one, say, on Lake Texoma, if you can forget that the affable hostess is the First Lady of the land. And except for the thrill and excitement of the occasion, I might even have forgotten that Mrs. Lyndon B. Johnson is that lovely and charming person.

On Sunday, October 25, 1964, I had the privilege of being one of approximately two hundred women from national and local news media who spent three hours as guests of Lady Bird on the LBJ Ranch, ten miles from Johnson City, Texas. Our credentials were checked as we entered the north gate of the ranch, and upon arriving at the scene of the gala affair we were met by "Ladies for Lyndon" hostesses who put everyone in the mood for the occasion with red western handkerchiefs and "LBJ for USA" straw hats with red, white, and blue ribbons.

Mrs. Johnson greeted each guest individually and presented her to her houseguests and traveling companions: Mrs. Robert McNamara, wife of the Secretary of Defense; Mrs. John Connally, wife of the governor of Texas; Mrs. Orville Freeman, wife of the Secretary of Agriculture; and Mrs. Willard Wirtz, wife of the Secretary of Labor. Mrs. Johnson and the honorees could not have been more charming or made anyone feel more at home than these women did in greeting the guests, who, like myself, were a little awe-struck. After picture-taking sessions, we were seated at tables for eight, which were marked with such banners as "Lady Bird Special."

Mrs. Johnson, Mrs. Connally, and the wives of the Cabinet members, who that day began an 868-mile hop-skip campaign swing by plane through Texas, then stepped onto the speakers' platform for a "speech-making session."

Mrs. Johnson welcomed the members of the press to the LBJ Ranch and introduced her houseguests, whom she planned to show the three faces of Texas—industrial, farming, and cattle country. She began Sunday morning by taking the group with her to church in Fredericksburg, where they attended services at St. Barnabas Episcopal Church, built in 1848.

Mrs. Connally, who joined Mrs. Johnson for the campaign trip aboard the "Lady Bird Special," provided an official welcome to Texas. Mrs. Johnson reminded her guests that her flying trip through Texas was designed to help "elect the Democratic ticket from the courthouse to the White House."

Mrs. McNamara, who was instrumental in beginning a widespread remedial reading program in Washington, D.C., told how impressed she had been by the concern for education shown by the Democratic administration.

In describing research work done by the government in centers such as Beltsville, Maryland, near Washington, in the development of wash-and-wear fabrics, shipping, and freezing and dehydrating foods, Mrs. Freeman said that the services rendered by the government in "helping people to help themselves" is a great joy to her.

Mrs. Wirtz, a member of the President's Committee on Employing the Handicapped, lauded Texas for its program of hiring handicapped persons. She said that working with this twenty-year-old committee, of which Mrs. Johnson is honorary chairman of the women's subcommittee, "has become a most rewarding hobby."

Among other well-known persons present was Dr. Janet Travell, personal physician of the late President John F. Kennedy. Mrs. Johnson said that Dr. Travell went for a 6:30 A.M. swim Sunday in the ranch pool. Other notables included Mrs. Clifford Davis, head of the Women's Speakers Bureau for the Democratic

Party; Mrs. Eugene Locke of Dallas, national committeewoman for Texas, who joined the group on the flight today; and Mrs. Jerry Williams of Austin, state coordinator of Texas Democratic women's activities.

Mrs. Williams said, "Never before have so many women taken such an active part in the Democratic campaign." She said that for the first time in history, the Democrats have a woman coordinator in each of Texas' 254 counties. She announced that Texas women will begin a "Tell a Friend" telephone program on October 20, with Mrs. Connally making the first call.

Mingling with the crowd of women and a few male reporters were Mrs. Johnson's constant traveling companions, a group of neatly dressed Secret Service agents, who kept a sharp eye on the happenings. Several stood around the speakers' platform watching with more interest the large crowd of sightseers that gathered across the river at the main road. A constant stream of lookers drove by the ranch.

Barbecued beef, shrimp, and chicken with beans, slaw, potato salad, corn on the cob, hot home-made biscuits, hot fried pies, and Texas-sized mugs of iced tea and coffee were served within easy sight of the LBJ Ranch home.

Walter Jetton of Fort Worth, the "Leonard Bernstein of the barbecue world," who has been barbecuing for the Johnsons, including Luci and Lynda, during the campaign, served the typically Texan feast. Also assisting was Mrs. Esther Coopersmith of Washington, who has been arranging all of the barbecues for Luci and Lynda across the land.

We were entertained as we ate by Trio Los Amigos; Marina Ecos de Cheapas of Laredo; television personality Cactus Pryor; folk singer Carol George of El Paso, who is doing the background music for a movie on the life of President Johnson; and University of Texas psychology major, Ricardo Gomez of San Antonio, who is becoming well known for his guitar ability through recordings and as a Six Flags attraction.

Texas "Ladies for Lyndon" helped greet everyone and conducted tours through the ranch home. They were dressed in their specially designed "bluebonnet blue" dresses that were topped with fringed ponchos monogrammed with the initials "LBJ."

During the tour through the home, we saw pieces of Mrs. Johnson's copper collection; President Johnson's stuffed deer heads, where several of his hats were hanging; the well-staffed kitchen, where two enormous pecan pies were cooling for the evening meal; and the President's office. A life-sized portrait was hanging over the mantle in this office, and the saddle presented to LBJ by President Adolfo Lopez Mateos of Mexico was in prominent view. That was a fitting end to such an exciting and memorable afternoon.

Fig. 19. Donna Hunt, left, women's news editor of The Denison Herald, *chats with Mrs. Lyndon Johnson at the LBJ Ranch, at a barbecue the First Lady hosted for newswomen.*

13

Assassination of John F. Kennedy

November 22, 1963.

It began as a normal workday at *The Denison Herald*. Wire editor Byron Buzbee was taking his regular Friday off, and Editor Claud Easterly was handling the wire. The paper, filled with happy news about U.S. President John F. Kennedy's visit to Dallas—just 75 miles south of Denison—had been closed out. The news staff, with the exception of the young women's editor, had gone to lunch.

I was that young women's editor.

Just after 12:30 P.M., the bell on the old Associated Press wire machine, which usually jingled to alert the editor of a bulletin, went crazy. I walked to the machine to see what had set off the bothersome noise. What I saw was hard to absorb. The bulletin read simply: "DALLAS (AP) — President Kennedy was shot at noon today."

My first reaction was panic. But I ran to the back shop, where the paper was being put together, and yelled, "Stop everything, the President's been shot!" Everyone made a run for the AP machine to see for themselves this unbelievable news.

Then I called Claud Easterly, who was having lunch at home. When he answered the phone, I said, "Mr. Easterly, President Kennedy's been shot."

All I heard was "Oh my God," followed by the slam of the telephone. Easterly later said that that day at noon was the only time in his newspaper career lasting forty-plus years that he ran red lights to get to a story.

By the time he arrived back in the newsroom, people off the street who heard the announcement on their car radios or on television were stopping by the office (then located upstairs in the original part of the building at 331 West Woodard Street). Updates were coming over the wire as fast as they could be typed at AP headquarters in Dallas. The little bell was ringing almost constantly. Telephones were ringing. Everyone was asking two questions: How was the President? and Who did it? Like the rest of the world, we had no answers.

The front page was made over using information on the bizarre happenings in Dallas. Background information on Kennedy's trip to Texas and events of the morning were hurriedly put together.

Then came the AP message that will never be forgotten: "DALLAS (AP) — President Kennedy died at 1 P.M. (CST)."

At the Dallas Trade Mart, where hundreds of supporters had assembled to hear the President speak, *The Herald's* publisher, Fred Conn, heard the word that the President wasn't coming—would never come. He immediately began to make his way back to Denison.

Grayson County Sheriff Woody Blanton was in Dallas with a rifle taken for a ballistics test. He later admitted that he had a few anxious moments when he heard on his car radio that his fellow lawmen were looking for a suspect with a rifle.

On that day, *The Herald* was able to get what facts and photographs were available and still go to press only a few minutes late. Once the day's paper was well on its way for a second time that day, those of us who had not had lunch battled the butterflies in our stomachs and went to the old Eat-Well Cafe on Main Street, where owner Carl McCraw had set up a television for the downtown crowd to join the world in the start of a four-day television marathon.

We watched as Lyndon Johnson was sworn in as President, with Jackie Kennedy standing by his side. We watched as world leaders assembled in Washington, D.C., for a final salute to the fallen President. We even watched in horror as Dallas nightclub owner Jack Ruby stepped out from the crowd at Dallas Police Headquarters and shot Lee Harvey Oswald, who had been arrested as the President's assassin.

Yes, November 22 and the three days following are printed indelibly in the minds of all who watched. And for those of us who feel we were involved—no matter how minutely—in the happenings of those days, it was a time that we'll never forget.

Fig. 20. President John F. Kennedy arrives at Perrin Field, Denison, to attend funeral of Sam Rayburn in Bonham, Texas, 1961. Photo by Claud Easterly for The Denison Herald. *Courtesy of Billy Holcomb.*

Fig. 21. Claud Easterly was for many years editor of The Denison Herald. *He hired Donna Hunt as a young typesetter and soon recognized her ability as a writer, giving her increasing responsibility over the years.*

14

Claud Easterly, Boss and Mentor

Claud Easterly was my boss for many years and my mentor for many subsequent years after he retired in 1971. He knew more about Denison's early years than most anyone in town.

Both Claud and Ruth Easterly were born in Denison and graduated from high school together in 1925. Ruth went to Austin College, where she majored in Spanish, with the appropriate education courses to be a teacher. She taught Spanish for a brief period in Denison, then became a stay-at-home mom after her son David was born. She died in 1967.

Claud came from modest means, with his father frequently out of work. His mother took in sewing. In the early 1920s, Claud's father worked at the Katy Shops. When interviewed by my uncle, judge and historian R.C. Vaughan, Claud remembered the Railroad Strike of 1922. More than 1,400 employees in Denison joined the national strike. Denison was put under martial law, with 500 soldiers of the Texas National Guard patrolling the town and camping in Forest Park. Families turned against families when some of the employees decided to return to work. In July, 47 workers arrived aboard a Katy train to replace some of the shop employees who were on strike. A group of these workers, called "scabs," were seized and taken across Red River, beaten, and then turned loose with orders not to return to Denison.

Mr. Easterly's father was one of the strikers who never returned to the Katy Shops. He knew something about carpentry and took up that trade. Had Mr. Easterly's mother not been a good seamstress, he said, the family would have gone hungry.

After graduation from Denison High School, Claud went to work at *The Denison Herald* at no pay until he learned the job. Three months later, on August 31, 1925, he was put on the payroll at a salary of $12.50 a week. He was named editor in 1942.

During his career, Claud covered the Red River Bridge War in 1931, which ended just in time for him to make it to the church for his wedding to Ruth Davis. In the 1940s, he covered an photographed the construction of the Denison Dam; and in 1944 he covered the butane explosion in Denison that killed thirteen people. He interviewed five U.S. Presidents, even more vice presidents, Speaker of the House Sam Rayburn, legendary bandleader John Phillip Sousa, magician Harry Houdini, Father Flanagan of Boys Town, New York Mayor Fiorello LaGuardia, heavyweight boxing champion Joe Louis, and many other dignitaries. He traced the end of the MK&T Railroad and the closing of passenger train service in Denison. His newspaper career spanned 47 years.

It was at Denison High School that he developed his love for writing when he excelled in an English class. When the school newspaper was searching for an editor, his English teacher recommended him for the job. He became editor of the *Denison Hi Buzz*. Fifty years after graduation (at which Sam Rayburn had been the commencement speaker), Claud's class chose him to be master of ceremonies at its fiftieth reunion.

His ethics in writing were above reproach, and those who worked on his staff always will remember his fairness to his employees and to the public. He never sought the limelight and preferred to stay at his desk as working editor of a small newspaper. He never lost his zest for even routine stories.

Mr. Easterly (I never could call him Claud as he requested) knew and interviewed many of the founding fathers of Denison and was the last connection between the current generation and the actual founders.

David Easterly followed in the footsteps of his father by pursuing a newspaper career after graduating from Denison High School in 1960. His dad was so proud of him as he progressed up the ladder to become President and CEO of Cox Newspapers in Atlanta, Georgia. After retiring from his post with Cox, he served on the board of Cox Enterprises Inc.

After his dad died on March 15, 1999, David established the Claud Easterly Foundation, into which he placed his dad's estate. Additional funds have also been added.

In 2006 David established a Memorial Scholarship Program with the Denison Education Foundation to honor both his mother, Ruth Davis Easterly, and his father. David said he knew that his dad would be excited to know that he was able to help children with financial needs to further their education and to succeed in life. David said his parents believed strongly in education and were committed to helping the community in any way possible. He said the scholarships in their name benefitting Denison children seemed the perfect way to honor the many significant contributions they made to Denison.

There is no doubt that they would be proud.

Fig. 22. Claud Easterly began his career in journalism as editor of Denison High School's student newspaper, The Buzz.

Fig. 23. Donna's
years at The
Denison Herald
*included a lot of
work and also
plenty of fun. See
her (above) at her
desk, and (right)
getting to know a
visiting leopard who
stopped by the office
while in Denison.*

Herald photo by David B. Stevens

Denison Herald Editor Donna Hunt gets acquainted with
Tanya, an Indian leopard which dropped by the newsroom Friday for an interview.

15

Not a Quitter

I don't like to think of myself as a quitter, but I did resign at *The Denison Herald* a number of times. I believe it was in 1957 when I first went to work on a newspaper, the *Sherman Democrat*, mostly as a proofreader and also as a teletype setter. I'll tell you more about quitting a little later.

The only writing experience I had in high school was on the newspaper and the yearbook, and I had loved it. I applied at the Sherman paper because I needed a job, and "proofreader" sounded like it would be pretty easy. I was wrong, but I loved working in the composing room anyway.

After about a year, Claud Easterly, editor of *The Denison Herald*, called me and said he had heard that I had some teletype experience. I told him that I had very little and that my primary job had been proofreading. He said that he would like to talk to me. Since I lived in Denison, I decided that it would be better to work there, so I took the job that Claud offered me.

The day I was supposed to go to work teletype setting, the women's news (then called "society") assistant quit, and I was asked to fill in until they could hire someone. The primary responsibility was making "brief runs" twice a day—going downtown a block away and canvassing the businesses for short items about visitors, birthday parties, and such. I also helped the society editor write club news and even obituaries.

About six months later, the society editor went on to bigger and better things, and I was promoted to her position. I really felt important. At that time, I covered a lot of women's club meetings with my hat and gloves on. I also took a lot of club news reports over the telephone. I took so many that I developed a crick in my neck and had to go to the chiropractor. Then I managed to get a headset to solve the problem.

Weddings were something we went all out on, and in June especially I was very busy writing all the wedding stories. Some Sundays I didn't even have room for all of them.

I had to learn to operate a 4x5 camera with either flashbulbs or a very heavy battery pack on my shoulder. I did not cover weddings, however, but soon began shooting wedding pictures for a fee when asked.

This wasn't a bad job for a 22-year-old just out of high school, with less than a year of college working toward a business degree. The pay wasn't much, but no one's pay was great in those days. I think I made something like $30 a week, and when I got a raise, it was a nickel an hour.

While I was the society editor, I also helped with obituaries and occasionally wrote general news stories. I even learned to engrave photos on the giant machine near my desk in the newsroom.

I neglected to say that I was married when I went to work at *The Herald*. A couple of years later, I found that I was pregnant. Still, I worked almost until my oldest son was born. The staffers kept telling me they were going to get me a basket to put him in so I could just keep working. But I had thoughts of staying home with him, so I quit for the first time. But circumstances didn't dictate my staying at home, so six weeks after Rob was born, I asked for and was given my job back.

Then, about fourteen months later, I was pregnant again and went through the same routine of quitting to stay home with the two babies. But it was only a dream, and I went back to the newspaper a second time.

The editor, Claud Easterly, turned out to be my mentor and taught me how to write feature stories and what we called "weekly cooking features." He critiqued every feature I wrote and seldom hurt my feelings.

After fourteen years, dealing with women began to get the best of me, and writing about weddings became boring. By that time, I was on the board of the Denison Camp Fire Girls. When the executive director retired, I quit *The Herald* again and took her job for three years. But printer's ink gets into your blood, and I never felt at home with all those beautiful little girls.

When the editor of *The Denison Herald* retired, the city editor, John Crawford, was named editor and began looking for a new city editor. He called me, and once again I went to work for the paper, this time as city editor. We had a staff of twelve, including reporters, a photographer, wire editor, two in sports, two in women's news, the editor, and me. I still covered a lot of meetings, such as the school board and city council, while directing the operation of the newsroom. I loved it until John Crawford resigned to become publisher of another newspaper out of our area.

An editor was hired who had no idea what he was doing. By that time, I was pretty much running the newsroom and had to train him. This didn't set too well, but it was a fact of my job. He didn't last too long in his position, and ten minutes after he turned in his resignation, I was offered the job of editor.

The Herald had never had a woman as editor, and I, without a college degree, had never thought about becoming one. Fortunately, the town folks welcomed me with open arms. The day I took over, my office was full of flowers, and I had letters from many people, including our representatives in Congress and the Texas Legislature, Denison's mayor, and many others.

I loved my job. *The Denison Herald* was owned by Harte-Hanks Newspapers, and the company believed in training. I was sent to many workshops and took advantage of every opportunity to learn something to make my job easier. The staff was more like a family, and when something happened, we all pulled together to put out a good edition as close to deadline as possible.

One day we got word that the newspaper was being sold to Donrey Media Group, which also owned the *Sherman Democrat*. We were friendly with the *Democrat* people, but the two staffs were fiercely competitive. Editors of both papers were quick to scan the opposition paper every day and comment on stories we had missed or those that the other paper had missed. It made for a healthy rivalry until we were bought by Donrey Media.

The Herald's publisher, Jerry Crenshaw, had just learned that he had cancer, and the blow of being sold devastated him. He died within the year, and another Donrey publisher was brought in. He looked at the bottom line more than at the quality of the product. Training for staff was stopped, bonuses were eliminated, several people lost their jobs, and morale got pretty low.

I could see what was going to happen next—the two newspapers were going to be combined into one paper. The citizens of Denison were concerned that they were going to lose their paper, and every day I was asked what was going to happen. As the merger became imminent, I decided that I didn't want to be part of the transition.

At that time, Texas Rural Communities was managing the Dwight D. Eisenhower Birthplace State Historical Park in Denison. When I was approached about a position as director of the park, I decided to take the job and try to put the site on the map. So I quit *The Denison Herald* for the last time.

I loved working at the park doing marketing, planning events on special occasions, and working with President Eisenhower's granddaughters. When Texas Rural Communities returned the park the to Texas Parks and Wildlife Department, I was asked by Andy Sansom, TPWD executive director, to stay on as manager.

I didn't fit the criteria set for park managers. Later I was told that I was an executive appointment and they had a hard time finding a niche for me. Still, the TPWD was good to me and sent me to many, many training sessions. I did everything but carry a gun like the park rangers did. At one training sessions with about thirty park rangers, all carrying guns, I was the only woman. The speaker asked me where my gun was, and I told him that I wasn't allowed to carry one. He said that, given the crowd I was hanging out with, I needed one.

Being away from the newspaper was an interesting experience. I was able to write feature stories about the park, some of its visitors, and events we sponsored. We received some good publicity around the state from editors I had been friends with while working at *The Denison Herald*, and from magazines such as *Texas Monthly* and *Texas Highways*.

In June 2000, a day came that I had been anticipating for many years. I was old enough to retire but not really ready to sit down in a rocking chair. I had always thought that I would quit writing when I retired. But that didn't happen.

Right after I retired, a company established a weekly newspaper in town, the *Denison Post*. The editor and his wife were running the paper and asked me to help a couple of days a week. After a few weeks of freedom, I decided that I could use the extra cash and would like to get my feet wet once again. A year after the paper began weekly publication, it went daily. I didn't want that much work, though, so I just wrote columns and occasional feature stories.

The Denison Herald and the *Sherman Democrat* had merged to form the *Herald Democrat*. About a year after the *Post* went daily, the *Herald Democrat's* editor called and offered to buy me lunch. He asked me to come to work for his paper, writing columns at my leisure. I jumped at the chance. I resigned from the *Post*, which folded a couple of months later—though not because I left.

I had developed a special interest in the history of my area, and that was primarily what I had written for the *Post*. This had begun in 1976, when I won a Harte-Hanks Bicentennial trophy for the best historical column that year of our nation's 100th birthday. The editor and I decided that I would write two columns a week, mostly about area history, with special assignments that might come along.

In my new position, I went back to work with many old friends. I could do my work at home, whenever I wanted to, even at night in my pajamas if I chose. As of this writing in mid-2015, I have been writing these columns since 2002.

All this is a round-about way of saying that you can do what you want or need to do and have a great time. The pay isn't that great—it never was—but I don't know of a career I would rather have followed.

Beginning in 2009, I began leaning in another direction. With Dr. Mavis Anne Bryant, a friend who also follows Denison's history, I have written three books—one about our 1914 high school that was demolished under protest, another a pictorial history of Denison, and the most recent about Denison's early days as a frontier town.

Earlier in my life, no one ever would have been able to convince me that at age 79, I would still be writing and involved in a new angle of journalism, but that's where I stand. I've loved most all of it, and I've never regretted taking the paths that I have.

My word to anyone who is unhappy doing what he or she is doing is to look around. Take a chance, find something you love, and go toward it. You never know what direction that might point you.

Fig. 24. Newspaper headlines and Donna in new position at the Eisenhower Birthplace State Historical Park.

16

Front Yard Visitors

Spring and summer are a wonderful time of the year, especially if you live in the country. Every day there's a new show right in the front yard. It's wonderful to have the time now to enjoy it. The older I get, the more I enjoy watching birds—usually from the kitchen or dining room window—as they stop by to eat from one of several feeders in the front yard, get a drink or splash around in a birdbath nearby, or perch in one of the trees for a rest.

A good friend has arrived for its annual spring-summer visit. Actually, I think this little friend is a scout sent out to look around for a good place to camp. When we first saw it a couple of weeks ago, we were not prepared for its arrival.

When we went to the kitchen to put the coffee on one morning, a tiny hummingbird fluttered outside our kitchen window where we normally have a feeder for the beautiful little birds.

That was the signal to get ready in a matter of minutes for the arrival of others.

Each year our hummingbird feeder hangs in front of the window on the front porch, and generally from one to four "hummers" can be seen at all times of the day drinking and sometimes fighting over a favorite spot.

They can fight with such ferocity that if they were large birds, they could be dangerous. Yet at our house the larger birds seem to leave them alone. They probably couldn't catch them if they wanted to. It's amazing to watch their tiny wings flutter so fast and how they zoom to and from a nearby tree to take on nourishment.

While it would be impossible to count them, I've read that hummingbird wing beats are about 80 per second in forward flight and up to 200 per second when they are courting other hummingbirds. The heart rate for a hummingbird is about 1,260 beats per minute, according to researchers.

I've heard that scouts arrive early, and I think that's who is already at our house. Scouts are sent ahead of the rest of the crew to see where they are welcome and where feeders exist. If this is true, I hope our visitor informs his friends that we are ready for them, because they are such a delight to watch. I'd like to post a sign in the yard—"Hummers Welcome"—since they certainly are.

After a little research on hummingbirds, I learned that early settlers from Europe thought they were a cross between an insect and a bird when they first saw them. They couldn't figure out how so much life could come from such a small bundle of feathers.

The birds have been a part of Native American culture from the very beginning and have been copied in decorations, ceremonials, and mythology.

Christopher Columbus wrote of hummingbirds in his diary, and a few years after he discovered the New World, a hummingbird skin found its way to Rome as a gift to the Pope. Pope or not, I don't particularly like that story from Columbus' day.

They were called "flybirds" by early biologists, as they attempted to catalog and describe the world's hummingbirds.

The hummingbirds we see around here generally begin their migration in March from Central America, where they spent the winter. More than half come through Texas, some through Cuba and Florida, and some directly over the Gulf of Mexico. Contrary to what some believe, hummingbirds do not hitch rides on geese or other large birds. While research information talks about them going further north, some prefer to stay in Texas despite the heat.

I know we worried about our hummers last year and kept plenty of hummingbird food out for them. We were afraid they had become so comfortable that they wouldn't migrate with the rest of the birds, but when their time came, they went on their way. Information I've found said they arrive in the spring when food plants are blooming, and their departure coincides with the end of the blooming season in late July up north and late October in our part of the country.

We keep food out year round for the birds and for squirrels number 1, 2, 3, or 4. We even have a small squirrel feeder nailed on a tree in the front yard so that they can eat corn and other food without getting wet when it rains. And they've used it very often during our wet spring.

Our biggest problem has been keeping them out of the bird feeders. I think it has become a game with them. We move the feeder so they "cannot" get in it, and they figure out a way to get there anyway. We think they actually live in a neighbor's yard because we have dogs and cats, but every morning we see them scurry across the road to reach the squirrel feeder or to ponder how to get to the birdseed. They are cagey creatures and can scamper up a tree for protection at the slightest sound or movement.

Unfortunately, one of the cats occasionally sneaks up on one of our feathered friends, but that's a chance the birds have to take. Scolding the cat does no good. The dogs just like to give chase and wouldn't know what to do if they caught one.

Fig. 25. Donna Hunt with sons Brian and Rob.

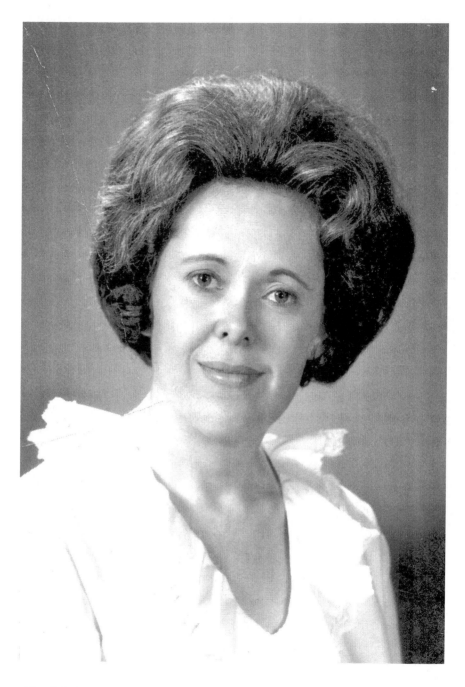

Fig. 26. Donna Hord Hunt, ca. 1957.

17

"Girls' Morning Out" Train Trip

Once you reach a certain age, everyone thinks that you have all the time in the world. It's not so! Friends and relatives come up with things for you to do since you're retired now and have all that spare time. But every woman (and man) needs a day out once in a while, away from the regular grind of housework, cooking, car-pooling, and all the other chores that generally keep us busy.

Every other Tuesday morning (every Tuesday for one group whose members are a couple of years older than our group), about seven or eight women who graduated from Denison High School in 1953, along with a couple who graduated in different years, get together for breakfast and to try to solve the problems of the world.

Unlike some of our husbands, who do this every morning and most times every afternoon, we get our talking done in a much shorter time. The older group that usually has 10 to 20 diners gathers in the back room at Nick's Restaurant every Tuesday at 8 A.M. to eat together and keep up with each other.

My classmates aren't such early risers, and we congregate about 9:30 A.M. and sometimes have to gently nudge our older friends out of a chair to have a place to sit together. Lavada Cuthbertson even brings cake for breakfast dessert every time we meet. On the Tuesdays when we don't get together, her sister, Billie Crook Jennings, Class of 1951, takes cake for the early-rising bunch. During a recent breakfast session, Carol Yelton mentioned taking the TAPS bus to Plano, then going to Union Station in

Dallas via the DART electric train to board the Texas Railway Express and go on to Fort Worth.

Someone said, "We should do that." Since every other Tuesday morning is reserved for "girls' morning out," we decided to enlarge upon that treat and take Carol's suggested jaunt. No one mentioned at that time that the TAPS buses leave the Wal-Mart parking lot in Denison at 5:30 and 6:30 A.M.

But we decided to rough it, and six of our group showed up not on time, but early, because we didn't want to miss the bus that leaves promptly on time. We picked up a seventh friend, Lavada, in Sherman after joining the early morning regulars, some of whom felt like we had invaded their domain and interrupted their morning routine. In addition to Lavada and Carol, our group was comprised of Alice Schick, Billie, Carolyn Greer (Class of 1954), Bettye Henry, and this writer.

After one more stop at Grayson County College's branch campus in Van Alstyne, we hit the road again and joined the morning commute crowd. Our driver was a pretty patient guy, but by the time we hit McKinney, traffic was backed up almost to the northern city limits. We were sure that he had encountered this kind of traffic many times before, as he exited the highway and took to the service road and tooled right on through McKinney with no problem. I must remember to do that.

We arrived at Parker Road and the DART station in Plano in an hour and a half and were greeted by a sea of cars belonging to train commuters. Timing was perfect and we only had to wait a few minutes for the 47-minute ride on the Red line to Union Station. Here again we only had a few minutes to wait until it was time to board the red, white, and blue Trinity Rail Express train.

Actually, riding the DART electric train was almost like riding the Interurban of days gone by. It rocked and rolled on down the track, stopping at designated stations along the way. It even went underground and made up for lost time for several miles.

A word of warning: if you plan to take your own car to catch the train, the Parker Road station is a good place to begin, because it has parking available. While the train stops at various stations, most do not have parking facilities. Check it out before you go.

In case you're wondering what all this costs, it is the biggest bargain I've found in a long time. TAPS Bus to Plano is $4 each way, much less than gasoline would have cost us. But the biggest bargain was the train rides. Being the senior citizens that we are, we put $1 into the machine after we figured out how to work it and received a ticket good for the entire trip, including a Fort Worth transit bus to the Stockyards, where we ate lunch. If you decide to drive to the DART station and you are a senior citizen, the trip will cost you only $1 in addition to the cost of gas.

By 11 A.M. we were on the bus in Fort Worth, headed north to the stop about four blocks from the yards. After strolling down the hill looking at all the famous western stars' names inscribed in the sidewalk we wondered why all of the tourists were sitting or standing on the curbs in front of the shopping and restaurant area. Once we were seated in Ricky's Barbecue Restaurant we found out the reason. They were smart enough to know that the twice-daily cattle drive was due to appear at any time.

We may have missed the cattle drive, but we saw plenty of cowboys on horseback talking to the tourists and posing for pictures with them. They were kept busy by a large contingent of young Japanese boys and girls who really chowed down on Texas barbecue while seated with the guys at one end of the long outdoor table and the girls at the other end.

Two men nearer our age who sat next to us in the restaurant had ordered barbecue rib plates. When their food arrived we couldn't help but notice their surprise at the huge pile of ribs. The men, dressed in white business shirts and ties, quickly donned bibs to protect their clothes from barbecue sauce drips and dug in. When we left they were sacking up the bones for their dogs at home, and it looked like they did themselves proud by not leaving a whole lot for the pets. After a brief window-shopping stroll through the shops, it was time to climb back up the hill and begin retracing our steps back to Denison.

It was a longggg, fun day as we arrived back at our starting point a little after 7 P.M., but you can't beat $9 for 13 hours of togetherness. We're already trying to decide where we want to go next time. For now, though, it's back to breakfast and dessert next week. We welcome any former classmates to join us.

Fig. 27 (right). Donna Hunt at work.

Fig. 28 (below). Donna Hunt and Mavis Anne Bryant celebrate completion of the second book they produced together.

18

A Soldier Returns

Saturday was a special day for the Hunt family and at least 150 other families across the country. A military plane brought 151 soldiers into Dallas–Fort Worth Airport on their way home for a 15-day leave from their duties in Iraq.

On hand to welcome E-3 (soon to be E-4) Casey Hunt home was his mom, Vicky Weaver; sister, Nicole Hunt; and nephew, Dakota, all of Durant; and of course this writer, his grandmother, of Denison.

Excitement began building more than an hour before the plane arrived from Atlanta, Georgia, by way of Munich, Germany. By the time the plane arrived, the USO's greeting room was filled with family members, VetDogs and their trainers, Boy Scouts, Girl Scouts, and others who find pleasure in saying "Welcome Home" to their heroes.

A call to the USO Saturday morning told us that the plane was expected at 10:45 A.M. We had earlier been told it was to arrive at 11:50 A.M. It was about 8 A.M. when we learned of the arrival time change, and the rest of Casey's family was still in Durant. As we all ran out the door to face the grueling Highway 121 traffic to DFW, we decided to meet on Highway 75 to drive to together. By then it was 9 A.M., and frankly, I was worried we wouldn't get there in time.

Then the cell phone rang, and Casey said that they still were in Atlanta. We breathed a sigh of relief, and driving became a lot

81

easier. When we arrived at the airport, we were told they were expected about 11:40 A.M., but it was after 12 o'clock noon before the plane touched down. By then the room was filled.

Posters made by youngsters and adults in the Dallas-Fort Worth area lined the large room, and balloons printed with "Our Heroes," "Welcome Home," and lots of other wonderful messages decorated the big space. Baskets of cookies were provided by the USO, and everyone was eager for the announcement that the plane had landed.

When we first arrived, we spoke with four Dallas ladies dressed in red, white, and blue and holding American flags. These ladies didn't know anyone on the flight but were members of the William John "Bill" Bennett Fan Club. Bennett, former U.S. Secretary of Education under President Ronald Reagan, had a radio program that the women listened to regularly. They got together once a month and went somewhere, and one decided that greeting the returning military was the place to go this month.

Next we sat next to the Mike Copelands of Colbert, whose son, Chris, was coming home on leave too. Chris Copeland, a medic, was stationed with Casey at Camp Bucca near Umm Qasar in Southern Iraq, in what is supposed to be a "Green Zone." Both are with the Oklahoma National Guard as part of the 180th Infantry Brigade, 45th Division.

Chris' parents represented his family since Chris' wife Larissa was busy receiving her degree at Southeastern Oklahoma State University in Durant.

Casey, an MP (Military Police), is helping guard Camp Bucca, where hundreds of Iraqi prisoners are detained in a compound. He went to Iraq earlier this year and had been housed in a huge tent until last week, when he and others moved into barracks with four to a room, when others rotated home as their deployment ended. Life got a lot better with that move.

The surprise on the returning men's and women's faces as they turned the corner into the USO welcome center was something to see. Family members were given preference in the welcoming line, so that they could greet their returning soldiers as they entered the room.

Standing next to us were a set of parents, a very pregnant wife, and a son who looked to be about two years old. When "daddy" rounded the corner and the family screamed, the baby began reaching for his daddy, who also had tears in his eyes. The baby grabbed him around the neck and wouldn't let go.

Standing on the other side was a young woman from San Antonio, who had started driving at 3 A.M. to get to Dallas, rather than wait for her husband to catch another flight to go to San Antonio. She said they were married the Saturday before he left on Thursday and that was nine months ago. Needless to say, she was excited.

With camera poised, I waited to see our familiar face round the corner. When he did, I hardly recognized this young man, who had been more like a boy when he left. His mother saw him first and grabbed him around the neck for what seemed like minutes, before she turned loose for the rest of us to welcome him home.

The crowd formed a tunnel as soldiers and their families walked through the room to the sound of military marching music to head back to their homes. All along the way hands were held out to touch the soldiers, kind words were issued, and flags were waving. It was an awesome sight that I wish everyone could have an opportunity to witness and participate in. There were very few dry eyes.

Before the plane arrived, there were four black four-legged welcomers on hand that drew the attention of the crowd and posed for photographers, including this one.

The guys were Labrador Retrievers wearing jackets noting that they were guide dogs in training. Each also had on a red, white, and blue bandana. Holding their leashes were men and women wearing T-shirts designating them members of America's VetDogs, Veterans' K-9 Corps.

One who drew special attention was a pup three months old, who had been in training for only two weeks but acted far beyond his age and training period. His trainer said that she would have him for about a year before he is placed with a veteran needing his services.

I asked another young trainer with one of the beautiful dogs if it was hard to give them up at the end of their training. He said that "Liberty" was the fifth dog that he had trained; and, "Yes, it is really hard to see them go." Knowing where they are going and what they will be doing makes the pain go away, though.

No doubt the animals are taken to the USO's Welcome Home Center to help get them accustomed to crowds and noise. There was plenty of both in Dallas Saturday, but the dogs were part of the crowd and wagged their tails to offer their own welcomes. The VetDogs project is a new program from the Guide Dog Foundation for the Blind. I found lots of information about the project and how to become a part of it or how to receive a guide dog on the Internet by simply calling up VetDogs. You also can find the information at www.guidedog.org/Vetdogs.

Yes, Saturday was an exciting day for many soldiers' families. There is only one day that will be more exciting, and that's when the heroes return home to stay.

Fig. 29.
Donna's
grandson,
Casey
Hunt.

19

The Books Have Arrived!

The books have arrived!!! That's all I could think about on Thursday, when a call was received from Tina Hagburg in the Denison office of the *Herald Democrat*. The books, *Two Schools on Main Street: The Pride of Denison, Texas, 1873-2007*, had been anxiously awaited for several days.

Mavis Anne Bryant and I began writing this book almost eighteen months ago. That's twice as long as it takes for a baby to be born, and waiting for it to materialize at times has been pretty painful.

Long before we started writing, Mavis had mentioned to me several times that we should write a book about the high school that we both attended in the 1950s and that had just been demolished. One day she mentioned it again, and I told her, "Okay, let's do it."

Both of us are pretty good pack rats, but she's an organized one. We both had been accumulating information about our school and the one before it, so the first thing we did was put it all together. Maybe I should say that Mavis put it all together. I had a lot of files, but they weren't exactly in an order that made it easy to locate most anything.

Mavis dumped my files into a big box, took them home with her, and probably sat up most of several nights getting everything neatly packaged in plastic sleeves placed in extra-thick three-ring black binders.

When she returned with thirty-one of the fat notebooks that contained our merged information, my little home office next to the kitchen groaned when it saw her coming.

It was with all that research and lots more that we began writing well over a year ago, with the idea of having the book ready for distribution by Christmas. Mavis' brother, David Bryant, also a graduate of Denison High, agreed to back our venture and formed the Gate City Publishing Company to publish the book.

Next we hired a book designer to put the volume together. An August deadline was set for our part of the project to be completed, in order to have the book out by Christmas.

Both our computers began humming as we dug into the black notebooks and began telling the story of the beginning of education in Denison, soon after the town was established in 1872. We came up with a wealth of information that had never been assembled in one place before. Putting it all together was fun, as we saw how the Denison Educational Institute/Washington School came into being.

We began collecting pictures from many different sources, including local photographers; and we dug deeply into my historical Denison photo collection. I had always known that someday all those photos would come in handy.

After the town outgrew the 1873 school, the school as we knew it was built in 1913 and served as Denison High School, then McDaniel Junior High School, until it closed in 1986. That's all in the book, along with more than 200 photographs from the very beginning until the last brick fell in 2007.

Our book designer had a good idea, suggesting that we include every graduate whose senior picture appeared in any **DHS** yearbook as far back as we could find. You'll see 4,358 of those photographs grouped with their classmates.

Things went along beautifully, with Mavis and I typing away, reading each other's copy, and putting the pictures together with the story. We met our August deadline and began planning for the book's release before Christmas.

What is it they say about the best laid plans? The book designer and his wife had a few health issues, and he was unable to do the work as planned. So Mavis and I had to step in and take on a lot of the work that we hadn't planned to do.

Since Mavis is the technical person who also is a perfectionist of sorts, she worked with the designer to put the book together. It fell my lot to scan and work magic on those 4,358 photos, then group them into grids of 48 to a page. With instructions from our expert book designer, I sat at my computer for at least three months, working on photos. I feel personally acquainted with graduates all the way back to 1911. There were several years during the Depression and a few years earlier when yearbooks were not produced. Thanks to the records in the school administration building, we were able to at least get the names of those grads.

We were very careful to document everything we included in the book and are confident that everything in it is true and factual. Both Mavis and I are sticklers for getting the facts correct, and we've left no stone unturned.

You'll find the story of the clock, the bell, and the clock tower that later stood on the Woodard Street–Armstrong Avenue corner of the vacant city block where the schools were located for so many years. There's a chapter with remembrances written by an early founder of Denison and lots of former students, many of whom are no longer with us.

We covered the later years of the school that we all knew and loved, including desegregation, the school as a part of the Denison Commercial Historic District, and the building as a shell of the former school that many wanted to save but just couldn't come up with the funds to do it.

The last chapter is one that was the hardest to write, because so much emotion was generated in watching the building go from a "sacred site" to a pile of rubble.

Needless to say, the book wasn't finished by Christmas. We had to apologize to everyone who bought one as a gift. We worked as hard and as fast as we could, but there was just no way we could complete the task until well into 2009. We wrote a letter to that effect and placed one into each pre-ordered book. We signed all of those copies of the book and mailed them or left them to be picked up at the Denison office of the *Herald Democrat*.

We scheduled book signings where the books were available to purchase, and we were on hand to sign them. People stopped by to take a look at the 335-page book and relive some of the wonderful memories. It was great fun to hear people's recollections.

It was our wish—Mavis' and mine—that the book would be used for many years for research into the two schools and that families in the future could read it and look at the photos of their family members with pride.

Fig. 30. Donna Hunt celebrating the arrival of her first book, Two Schools on Main Street: The Pride of Denison, Texas, 1873–2007.

Appendix A

Life of Donna Hord Hunt

1935	June 7. Born in Denison TX. Parents: Lucious R. Hord and Inez Vaughan Hord.
1941–1953	Education in Denison public schools. Studied journalism in 11th and 12th grades.
1953	May. Graduated, Denison High School, in top 10 percent of class. Awarded Y-Teen Cup for Complete Womanhood.
1953–1954	Attended North Texas State University, Denton. Business major.
1954	March. Married in Denison, Texas.
1954–1956	Secretary, Perrin Air Force Base.
1956–1957	Teletype setter and proofreader, *Sherman (TX) Democrat*.
1957–1970	Women's Editor, *Denison (TX) Herald*.
1959	September 22. First son, Loy Robert, born.
1960	December 1. Second son, Brian Kent, born.
1962	Divorced.
1964	Guest of Lady Bird Johnson at LBJ Ranch, with large group of female dignitaries.
1965	Marriage to David R. Hunt in Hobbs NM.
1966	David R. Hunt legally adopts sons, 1966.
1969	Named "Girl of the Year" by Beta Sigma Phi.

Leadership Training with Camp Fire Girls, two weeks in Chicago.

Guest of Pillsbury at Pillsbury Bake-Off, Atlanta GA.

Tour of leading restaurants in Georgia as guest of Georgia Press Association.

1970 Luther Halsey Gulick Award; highest award given a volunteer by Camp Fire Girls.

Named "Outstanding Young Woman of Texas."

1970–1972 Executive Director, Denison Camp Fire Girls. Designed and directed a program for seniors at Sherman High School to prepare them for business in their future. Program used for several years.

1970–1981 Grayson County College. Courses in photography, history, general business, psychology, speech, sociology.

1972–1984 City Editor, *Denison Herald.*

1973 Harte-Hanks Newspapers Supervisory Program.

1976 Wrote weekly "Once Upon a Time" column for American Bicentennial.

First place, "Harte-Hanks Bicentennial Award" for best locally written column (history).

Chairman of writing and publishing *Texas Press Women's Cookbook.*

1984–1994 August 9, 1984, through March 1994. Editor, *Denison Herald.* 14,000 circulation daily newspaper. First female editor.

1986–1994 Harte-Hanks Newspaper Editorial Board. Served two years as contest director, member of Editorial Focus Board.

1980–1981 Dale Carnegie Training Course, 1980; graduate assistant, 1981.

1985 Named "Woman of the Year" by Denison Business and Professional Women's Club.

1986 One of 80 editors and broadcasters from across nation invited to White House by President Reagan for lunch and briefing.

1981	"She Knows Where She's Going" Award from Denison Girls Club.
1981	Helped establish Grayson County Women's Crisis Center for abused women and their children. Board member, 1981–1988.
1984	"Distinguished Service Award" from Denison Business and Professional Women.
1984–1985	President, Press Women of Texas.
1984–1986	"School Bell Award" from Texas State Teachers Association. 3 consecutive years.
1985	Helped organize Denison Leadership Institute, to train prospective community leaders.
1985–1990	Director, Herald Editorial Advisory Group.
1989	Named "Communicator of Achievement" by Press Women of Texas and National Federation of Press Women.
1990	"Athena Award" as outstanding female volunteer, Denison Chamber of Commerce.
	February 18. *Denison Herald* begins pictorial "Focus on Texoma" section.
1994	March 6. Donna Hunt Hord retires from *Denison Herald*.
1994–2000	March 1994 through June 2000. Manager, Eisenhower Birthplace State Historical Site, Texas Parks and Wildlife Department.
1995–1999	Various courses sponsored by Texas Parks and Wildlife Department, including grant writing, sexual harassment, cultural resources, tourism, and others.
2000	February. Texas "Woman of the Millennium" by National Federation of Press Women.
	Responsible for Orientation Video at Eisenhower Birthplace, "Denison: An American Hero's Journey Begins." Wins first place in National Federation of Press Women contest.
	Named "Woman of Achievement" for 2000 by American Association of University Women, Texoma Branch.

	June 6. Retirement from Eisenhower Birthplace State Historical Site.
	June 29. First column for *Denison Post.*
2000–2003	Writer, *Denison Post* newspaper.
2003	February. Last column for *Denison Post.*
	September 15. Publication of last issue of *Denison Post* newspaper.
	November. "Distinguished Alumni Award" from Denison Alumni Association.
2003	March 16, 2003, to present. Writer, *Herald Democrat.* Two history columns a week.
2008	"Achievement in Historical Writing Award," Grayson County Historical Commission. "Community Builder Award" from Denison's Billie Mosse Masonic Lodge 1152.
2009	First book published: *Two Schools on Main Street: The Pride of Denison Texas, 1873-2007,* written with Mavis Anne Bryant.
2011	Second book published: *Images of America: Denison,* written with Mavis Anne Bryant.
2015	Third book published: *Frontier Denison, Texas,* edited by Mavis Anne Bryant.
1957–2015	Numerous communications contest awards from Texas Press Association, Texas Press Women, National Federation of Press Women, Texas Associated Press Managing Editors, North and East Texas Press Association. Numerous speeches to civic and other organizations.

Appendix B

Local History Writings of Donna Hord Hunt (Through End of 2014)

The Denison Herald

1964

"Herald News Hen Rubs Elbows with Lady Bird at LBJ Spread: Herald Women's Editor Lady Bird's Sunday Guest," by Donna [Hord] Derebery [Hunt], Oct. 26, 1964.

"Personable Maryland Mother Plans Barbecues for LBJ Girls," by Donna [Hord] Derebery [Hunt], Oct. 29, 1964.

1967

"George's [Washington] Mail Believed Somewhere in Denison," Feb. 22, 1967.

"Martha Washington Buried Here: Old Doctor's Grave," July 30, 1967.

1968

"Clementine: A Small Story About a Large Pet," May 12, 1968.

"Dedicate Marker Today: Historic Thompson House Restored on Paw Paw Hill," June 9, 1968.

"Former Denison Girl [Janet Banzet] Blossoms Into New York Movie Starlet," date unavailable.

"Mystery in Oakwood [Cemetery]: Early-Day Denison Tombstone Deciphered," Apr. 7, 1968.

"Two Local Houses—Historic and Tarzan Style: William T. Lankford Home Built East of Town in 1847," Nov. 17, 1968.

1969

"Consider Historical Marker for Sand Springs: Watering Place for Pioneer Texans Still Bears Their Mark," May 11, 1969.

1970

"Shannon Cemetery May Be Denison's Oldest: Pre-Dates City by 24 Years," Oct. 18, 1970.

1971

"Denison Beginning 100th: Chaotic Beginning Recorded in Herald," Apr. 23, 1971.

1973

"Julie [Eisenhower] Highlights Statue Unveiling," July 10, 1973.

"St. Luke's Episcopal Church Celebrating Centennial Year," Oct. 21, 1973.

1974

"Driving in 1974 Not What It Used to Be," Apr. 28, 1974. J.L. Westbrook, early automobiles.

"Reunion: First and Last Y-Teen Cup Winners Meet in Denison," May 12, 1974.

"The Forum," Nov. 7, 1974. Public well, Alamo painting, teachers, George Washington's relatives.

"The Forum," Oct. 24, 1974. George Washington's relatives visit Denison.

"This Is Still Our Land," Sept. 15, 1974. Andrew Thomas and Lon Darwin families.

1975

"Do You Remember Pearl Harbor? These Men Do," Dec. 7, 1975. Allen Allender.

"Eisenhower Birthplace Manager [Emma Zander] Retiring After 17 Years," Apr. 6, 1975.

"[George] Washington's Camp Chest Found in London," Jan. 26, 1975.

"Graphic [Grayson County College] Takes On New Format, Leadership," Nov. 16, 1975.

"'Village Blacksmith' [Charles David Holden] Is 90," June 11, 1975.

1976 [American Revolution Bicentennial]

"Ancestor Ironsides Crewmember," Oct. 31, 1976. Martha Simms identifies relative.

"Bill's [Lawhon] Coffee Car," Jan. 25, 1976.

"City Unveils Katy Plaque: MK&T Historical Marker Dedicated," May 3, 1976.

"Local Surgeon [Stanley Clayton] Studies New Techniques in Colon Surgery," Nov. 21, 1976.

"Once Upon a Time," Jan. 11, 1976. First publication of a new column.

"Once Upon a Time," Jan. 18, 1976. William T. Lankford home.

"Once Upon a Time," Jan. 25, 1976. Old Settlers Association.

"Once Upon a Time," Feb. 1, 1976. Troop L, First Regiment, Texas Cavalry Volunteers, AKA Denison Rifles, in Cuba.

"Once Upon a Time," Feb. 8, 1976. Chinese in early Denison.

"Once Upon a Time," Feb. 15, 1976. Bell and clock tower at Historic DHS.

"Once Upon a Time," Feb. 22, 1976. Dr. L.A. Washington Jr.

"Once Upon a Time," Feb. 29, 1976. Mary Elizabeth Lease, local temperance movement.

"Once Upon a Time," Mar. 7, 1976. Dugan family, Indian fighting, skull.

"Once Upon a Time," Mar. 14, 1976. Kitching family, Indian fighting, Samuel Johnson.

"Once Upon a Time," Mar. 21, 1976. Butterfield Stage route, Sand Spring, Waterloo Lake.

"Once Upon a Time," Mar. 28, 1976. "Firsts," Euper's ice cream soda, UFOs.

"Once Upon a Time," Apr. 4, 1976. Chinese tombstone, Mary Elizabeth Lease, Samuel Johnson descendants, Butterfield Stage Route.

"Once Upon a Time," Apr. 11, 1976. Playwright Jay Turley, history of 1012 W. Main St.

"Once Upon a Time," Apr. 18, 1976. Denison's "Night of Terror," part 1.

"Once Upon a Time," Apr. 25, 1976. Denison's "Night of Terror," part 2.

"Once Upon a Time," May 2, 1976. Red River City; MK&T and H&TC railroads.

"Once Upon a Time," May 16, 1976. Andrew Thomas, Davy Crockett, Lon Darwin family.

"Once Upon a Time," May 23, 1976. James Kape Miller and Miller Spring.

"Once Upon a Time," May 30, 1976. Interurban and Woodlake.

"Once Upon a Time," June 6, 1976. Brief history of Denison, emphasis on statistics.

"Once Upon a Time," June 13, 1976. Lawson Lafayette Holder, Red River Flood of 1908.

"Once Upon a Time," June 27, 1976. Early Grayson County history.

"Once Upon a Time," July 4, 1976. Sophia Porter, Holland Coffee, Glen Eden.

"Once Upon a Time," July 11, 1976. Fourth of July festivities in 1876.

"Once Upon a Time," July 25, 1976. Red River Bridge War.

"Once Upon a Time," Aug. 1, 1976. Chronology of events, 1750 to 1896.

"Once Upon a Time," Aug. 15, 1976. Summer entertainment, property turnover.

"Once Upon a Time," Aug. 29, 1976. Sources of street names.

"Once Upon a Time," Oct. 3, 1976. Choctaw stoical when executed.

"Once Upon a Time," Oct. 17, 1976. Vin Fiz, first airplane to fly over Denison.

"Scrapbooks Hold Historic Memories," Sept. 19, 1976. Mrs. Vernon Beckham.

1977

"Cathey [Williams] Continues Rodeo in Father's [Mike Pribble] Memory," June 26, 1977.

"Crossing Red River Once Adventure; Colbert's Ferry Made Trip Easier," Nov. 27, 1977.

"Delaware Indians Established [Delaware] Bend in Red River," Nov. 10, 1977.

"Man [Carl McFarland] Researches [Pilot Knob Cumberland Presbyterian] Church Site," July 4, 1977.

1978

"Opera Houses Play Role in Early City," Apr. 12, 1978.

"The Older the Vehicle, the Better the Vintage," Dec. 10, 1978. Antique car buffs.

1979

"[B.] McDaniel's Notes Tell of School Designation," Sept. 2, 1979.

"Bells Toll for Last Time at Three Schools," May 6, 1979. Central Ward, Raynal, Peabody.

"Denison Has Fond Memories of Mamie's Visit," Nov. 1, 1979. Mamie Eisenhower.

"Denison Woman [Minnie Blake] Remembers Sophia [Porter]: Exhibit Opens Sunday at Sherman Museum," Aug. 24, 1979.

"Fateful July 4, 1879, Glorious, Tragic: Bloody Fourth, a Gala-Day of Horrors; Three Men Instantly Killed and One Wounded; Constable James Nelms One of the Victims; The Notorious Negro Desperado Charley Russell Killed," July 1, 1979.

"Grayson's First Court Session Held in Shade of Iron Ore Oak," Aug. 12, 1979.

"Historic [J.J. Fairbanks] House Filled With Many Memories" (part 2), Apr. 25, 1979.

"Jail on Wheels Joins Frontier Village Exhibit," Sept. 2, 1979.

"Memories of Sophia Porter Alive and Well," Aug. 12, 1979.

"Panoramic View," Sept. 9, 1979. 300 and 400 blocks W. Main St., 1916.

"They Said It Couldn't Be Done—But It Could" (part 3), Apr. 29, 1979. J.J. Fairbanks house.

"This Old [J.J. Fairbanks] House Is Going Downhill to a New Home" (part 1), Apr. 22, 1979.

1980

"Confederate Monument First in Texas: Monument Cornerstone Has History Documents" (part 1), July 6, 1980.

"County Can Rest With Knowledge That Courthouse Square Is Secure" (part 2), Sept. 7, 1980.

"Historic [William T.] Lankford House Rolls to New Home at Village," Jan. 27, 1980.

"[Jim Holland] Family Marks Anniversary of Immigration to America," Mar. 30, 1980.

"Meet the Golden Band from Jacket Land: The Band With a Beat," Oct. 5, 1980.

"Memories of Youth Ring Loud, Clear," June 25, 1980. DHS Class of 1953 reunion.

"Ridesharing—Who Says It's New?" May 28, 1980.

"Texas Barbecue Honors Hawaiian Cowboy [Fred Viveiros]," June 18, 1980.

"The 'Good Old Days' Had Their Own Fire Problems," Sept. 7, 1980.

"Top 1979 Stories Grab Headlines," Jan. 27, 1980.

1981

"Dec. 7, 1941—A Day to Remember, a Day to Forget," Dec. 6, 1981.

"Last War Between States Fought With Words, Not Bullets: Standoff at Red River Bridge," July 26, 1981.

"Recovery Complicated for Wounded Eagle," Jan. 18, 1981.

"Springs Flow Freely in Brune Book: Grayson's 22 Springs Included," Aug. 26, 1981.

"Wildlife Service Asks 'Who Shot Bald Eagle?'" Jan. 4, 1981.

1982

"$1 in 1882 Invested in Future—Today," Oct. 10, 1982. Forest Park.

"133-Year-Old [William T. Lankford] House Finds Permanent Home," Oct. 3, 1982.

"Block Gets Reprieve, Breath of New Life," Nov. 7, 1982. 100 block W. Main St.

"Buildings Reflect Progress: Then and Now," July 4, 1982. 401 W. Main St., 230 W. Chestnut St.

"Cars Park Where Rails Once Ran: Then and Now," July 11, 1982. 117-120 N. Houston Ave.

"CCD Center Replaces Regal [St. Xavier's] Academy: Then and Now," Aug. 8, 1982.

"Corner Makes Transition—Gas to Burgers: Then and Now," July 18, 1982. Northwest corner of South Austin Avenue and West Crawford Street.

"Denison Boasted First Skyscraper," Aug. 15, 1982. Security Building, 331 W. Main St.

"Denison's Night of Terror Remains Mystery: Murders Unsolved After 90 Years," May 16, 1982.

"Denisonians Have Been Cool Since 1876," Oct. 17, 1982. Crystal Ice Company.

"Justice System Expands from Shadetree to New Center," Sept. 12, 1982.

"Little [Virginia Point Methodist] Church's 145 Years of Roots Run Deep," Sept. 19, 1982.

"Local Man [Frank Donahue] Sees Job and Does It," Sept. 5, 1982. Clark Cemetery.

"Main Street Corner Grows With the City," Dec. 5, 1982. 300, 400 blocks W. Main St.

"McDaniel's [Junior High School] Past Colorful, Future Uncertain," Nov. 28, 1982.

"Office Supply Takes Kress Location: Then and Now," Aug. 29, 1982. 410 W. Main St.

"Old Fire House Charm Recaptured," Sept. 19, 1982. 320 W. Chestnut St.

"Post Office on Denison Scene Early: Then and Now," Aug. 1, 1982.

"Rod and Gun [Club] Early Hub of Social Activity," Oct. 31, 1982.

"Site of Famous [Eisenhower] House Beside Tracks Once Sold for 26 Cents," Sept. 26, 1982.

"Site of State's First Woman's Clubhouse," Dec. 12, 1982. XXI Club.

"Street Names Read Like History," Dec. 19, 1982.

"'Youngtimers' Also Remember Woodlake's Glamour," Nov. 21, 1982.

"You've Come a Long Way, Denison," Sept. 5, 1982. History of West Main Street.

1983

"Among Denison's First Needs—Law Enforcement," May 15, 1983.

"Art on Wheels," Feb. 27, 1983. Boxcar art.

"Baby, It Can Get Cold Outside in Denison," Jan. 30, 1983.

"Beadle Sees Denison as Quiet Railroad Town in 1873," Dec. 4, 1983.

"Books Available to Denisonians for Many Years," Jan. 23, 1983. XXI Club, Public Library.

"Business Rises From Central Ward [Elementary School] Rubble" (part 2), May 1, 1983.

"Central [Ward Elementary] Once Model Grammar School Building" (part 1), May 1, 1983.

"Christmas Eve 1872—A Beginning for the Katy's Baby," Dec. 25, 1983.

"City's Early [Hanna] Drug Store on Site of Present City Hall," Oct. 2, 1983.

"Denison Newcomers [Jean and Larry Lonis] Breathe Life Into Fairbanks House," June 26, 1983.

"Denison Plant [Levi Strauss] Sews Up Market Place in International 'Uniform'," Nov. 27, 1983.

"Denison Weather Has Ups, Downs," Aug. 14, 1983.

"Denison's First 'Grand Central Station' Had First Bar," July 24, 1983.

"Early Days of Denison Reflected in Munson Block," May 8, 1983.

"Early Denison Church [First Baptist] Faced Overpowering Challenge," July 17, 1983.

"Ferry Boat Once Carried Travelers Across Red River," June 12, 1983.

"First Newspaper Was Literally 'Red All Over'," Feb. 20, 1983.

"Former German Sea Captain Built [Travelers Hotel]," Aug. 21, 1983.

"Going Through Back Door to Texas-Oklahoma Exciting Ride," Mar. 6, 1983. Carpenters Bluff Bridge.

"Grocery Shopping in 'The Good Old Days' Was Different," Aug. 7, 1983.

"Historic Landmark [Cotton Mill] Goes Up in a Blaze of Glory," Jan. 16, 1983.

"In Its Heyday, Loy Lake Was the 'In' Place To Go," Feb. 27, 1983.

"Katy Depot Developers Start Feasibility Study," Aug. 21, 1983.

"Katy Depot Reflects Denison History," June 12, 1983.

"Katy Sells Landmark; Depot, Safeway Building Exchanged," May 31, 1983.

"Kiwanis Club Established Camp Fire Roots Here," Jan. 9, 1983.

"Memories of Early Day Business," Nov. 13, 1983. Elmer E. Davis Livery Stable.

"Methodist Church Has Its Start on Skiddy Street," June 5, 1983.

"Nov. 22, 1963: It Had Begun as a Normal Workday," Nov. 20, 1983. Assassination of John F. Kennedy.

"Quiet Denison [Oakwood] Cemetery Holds Key to Much History," Feb. 6, 1983.

"Rough and Rowdy Railroad Town Had Genteel Side," Mar. 13, 1983. Early churches.

"Rough, Rugged Denisonians Loved Ice Cream Soda," June 19, 1983.

"Strong People Helped Establish Pioneer Denison," Dec. 18, 1983.

"This Love Affair Has Lasted 60 Years," Aug. 21, 1983. Denison reunion in California.

"Those Were the Good Old Days," July 10, 1983. Businesses, ca. 1900.

"Transplanted Yankee Led Transition from Horse to Auto," Sept. 4, 1983. Elmer E. Davis.

"Travelers Today Keep Feet Dry Crossing [Red] River," Mar. 20, 1983.

"Village Cabin Gives Hint of Homelife in 1850," Mar. 27, 1983. Davis-Ansley cabin.

"Water Tower Gives Up Faithful Vigil Over [Cotton Mill] Building Ruins," Sept. 11, 1983.

"Yesterday's Headlines Record Today's History," Feb. 13, 1983.

1984

"A Hundred Years Ago: The Blacks in Blue," Apr. 27, 1984.

"Confederate Soldier Stands Guard Over Grayson Courthouse," Jan. 29, 1984.

"Crisis Line Gets Levi [Strauss] Grant: Battered Women's Shelter Opens," Nov. 23, 1984.

"DHS Band Marches in Eisenhower Inaugural Parade," Feb. 5, 1984.

"El Paso Artist [Bob Snead] Preserves Buffalo Soldiers," Apr. 27, 1984.

"Faithful Ex-Denisonians Remember," Nov. 11, 1984. Denison reunion in California.

"Fans Savor State Title: Santa Grants Christmas Wish," Dec. 24, 1984.

"Football Success Inspires Spirit," Dec. 9, 1984.

"Gigantic Sale Gives Future to Items from the Past," July 1, 1984. Nellie Chambers.

"Going, Going, Gone: Katy Depot Sold Without Auction," May 24, 1984.

"Historic Katy Railroad Depot on Threshold of New Beginning," May 20, 1984.

"Insistent Caller Changes Mind About Room," Oct. 28, 1984. Stardust Ballroom, Dan Fenton.

"Jacket Spirit Does Much for City," Dec. 16, 1984.

"Katy Plaza Gets Grant; Funding Contingent on Local Pledges," Aug. 15, 1984.

"Little-Known Denison College Provided Education for Blacks," Mar. 4, 1984. North Texas Baptist College and Seminary.

"New Column to Cover Movers, Moments," Oct. 7, 1984. First "Comments" column.

"'Old Gang of Mine' Has Baseball Reunion," Nov. 25, 1984. Cotton Mill Baseball Team, Pottsboro brothers in World War II, Yellow Jacket Band.

"Only God Can Make a Tree," Aug. 5, 1984. Maness and Nell Price, DBL Tree Acres.

"Papa Was a Veteran ... of the Civil War," June 11, 1984. Beulah Hull Riddle.

"Readers Can Expect Fair, Positive News Tone," Aug. 19, 1984.

"Sons' Graduations Keep Parents on Run," Dec. 30, 1984.

"Start Early, Take Time to Smell the Flowers," Oct. 14, 1984.

"The Lure of Gold Led to Man's [Leslie Franklin Clark] Discovery of an Old Bible," July 16, 1984.

"There's Humor Wherever You Look for it," Nov. 4, 1984.

"Well-Known Arizona Indian Captive [Olive Ann Oatman Fairchild] Traced to Sherman," Feb. 26, 1984.

"Yellow Jacket Spirit Inspires Citizens," Dec. 21, 1984.

1985

"A Lot of Hours Have Kept Camp Fire Growing," Jan. 27, 1985.

"Billboards to Proclaim [1984 Yellow Jacket] Championship," Apr. 14, 1985.

"CCC [Civilian Conservation Corps] Provided Opportunity to Make a Living," June 23, 1985.

"Clean Your Glasses, Halley's Comet Is Coming," June 30, 1985.

"Committees Gearing Up for [Texas] Sesquicentennial," Nov. 17, 1985.

"Cost of Property's Come a Long Way," June 2, 1985.

"Denison Artist's [Kate Whitehurst Hanna] Talent Unlimited," Nov. 24, 1985.

"Denison Man [Charles Dunning] Creates His Own Halley's Comet," Oct. 13, 1985.

"Denisonians Can Talk About Weather Again," Feb. 10, 1985.

"Denisonians KNOW [Joseph Anton] Euper Invented Soda," Nov. 24, 1985.

"Denisonians Preparing for Leadership Roles," Mar. 24, 1985.

"Drugs Seized at Denison Night Club [Lucille's]: Police Chief Says Drug Haul Largest in Denison's History," Sept. 16, 1985.

"Early Denison History Unearthed Downtown," Aug. 4, 1985.

"Former Denisonian [Rose Mary Badami] Helps Homeless," Feb. 17, 1985.

"George [Washington] Didn't Sleep Here, His Kin Did," Feb. 24, 1985.

"Golden Retriever Shares His Eyes with Owner [Carol Rainbolt]," May 12, 1985.

"Hats Off to You," Apr. 14, 1985. [First appearance of this column. It ran most weeks until June 22, 1986, citing area individuals and groups who deserve attention. Following that date, the column continued but did not carry Donna Hunt's byline.]

"Herald Reporters Go Remote," Mar. 10, 1985.

"[Herald] Staff Bids Good Luck to Sports Editor [T.R. Sullivan]," July 28, 1985.

"Historic Flight of Vin Fiz Remembered," Oct. 20, 1985.

"Ike Credited for Interstate System," May 5, 1985.

"Living on Easy Street" (Street Names, part 2), Sept. 1, 1985.

"Love Affair with Denison Still in Full Swing," Sept. 29, 1985. Denisonians in California.

"New Year's Resolutions 'Iffy'," Jan. 6, 1985.

"'Orange Blossom Special' Mystery Solved," Mar. 31, 1985.

"People, Places Gave Names to City Streets" (part 1), Aug. 11, 1985.

"Rodeo Not All Work for Bulls, Broncs," July 21, 1985.

"[Ross] Perot's Speech Gets Varied Reactions," Mar. 17, 1985.

"Rotarians Honor [Keith] Hubbard, [Marty] Criswell," Mar. 29, 1985.

"Teamwork Necessary in Playoff Coverage," Dec. 8, 1985.

"Texas Sesquicentennial Kicks Off in Grayson County," Apr. 14, 1985.

"Well-Known Santa's Helper [Tedd Riffell] Resting This Yule," Dec. 15, 1985.

1986

"Annie P. First Steamboat to Navigate Red River" ("firsts" part 2), Aug. 3, 1986.

"Baghwan's Rolls Royces Go On Auction Block," Nov. 23, 1986.

"Book Records Happenings of 1917 Class at Denison High," Apr. 20, 1986.

"Capsule Burial Ends [Texas Sesquicentennial] Celebration," Dec. 14, 1986.

"Denison Girl [Wendy Acree] Helps Save Lives of Wreck Victims," July 20, 1986.

"Denisonian [Janet Ciaccio] Among Regents at Republican Tea," May 25, 1986.

"Early Day Denison Mansion's Future Uncertain," Aug. 17, 1986. 412 W. Morton St.

"Faithful Graduates Make Frequent Returns for Reunion," Nov. 16, 1986.

"Favorite Relative [Tom Brown] Leaves Special Memories," Nov. 9, 1986.

"'Firsts' Contributed to City's Colorful Start" ("firsts" part 1), July 27, 1986.

"'For Life, I [Leta Koch] Am Thankful'," Nov. 27, 1986.

"Former Denisonian [Ruth Ann Overbeck] Now at Home in Nation's Capital," Feb. 16, 1986.

"Former Resident [Ray Clymer Jr.] Stands Up for Wichita Falls," Mar. 30, 1986.

"Hats Off to You," June 22, 1986. [Last time Donna Hunt's byline seen on this column.]

"Herald Reporter [Irene Flaherty] Applies for Space Mission," Jan. 26, 1986.

"Information Sought on Grayson Communities," June 15, 1986.

"Knights of Columbus Lobbied for 'Under God' in Flag Pledge," July 6, 1986.

"Leta Koch Fighting for Her Life," June 26, 1986.

"Let's Celebrate with a Party—Texas Style," Mar. 2, 1986.

"McAlester Brick Company Mystery Solved," Aug. 10, 1986.

"Meeting Old Friends Especially Nice in Summer," July 13, 1986.

"Most Journalists Still Would Go into Space," Feb. 2, 1986.

"No Longer Will Students Roam Halls of Old [High] School," June 1, 1986.

"Peanut Supply Company Sold," July 8, 1986. 114 N. Houston Ave.

"Remembrances of When ... Needed for Edition," Mar. 23, 1986. Katy Hospital.

"Sesquicentennial Workers Hold 'Stars of Texas' Party," Dec. 7, 1986.

"Texas Begins Gala Birthday Celebration," Jan. 5, 1986.

"'The Sesqui's [Sesquicentennial] Over,' Now What Can Be Done for an Encore?" Dec. 21, 1986.

"Train Send[s] Distress Signal to Sharp Eyes," Jan. 12, 1986. Upside-down flags.

1987

"38 of Every 100 Grayson Adults Illiterate," June 28, 1987.

"A Lot of Dreaming's Going On for Denison," Aug. 30, 1987.

"A Unique Publication," intro. to "Katy Railroad: At the End of the Line," Special Report, Dec. 13, 1987.

"At What Point Do You Become Elderly?" Aug. 9, 1987.

"BPW [Denison Business and Professional Women's Club] Throws Gala 50th Anniversary Party," Apr. 26, 1987.

"Brainstorming Brings Party 'For the Fun of It'," May 31, 1987. Allen Crenshaw.

"Capt. Santa Claus [N.J. 'Jesse' James] Reflects on Perrin's Past Christmases," Dec. 20, 1987.

"Denison Dam Scrapbook Collected with Love [by Fern House]," Dec. 20, 1987.

"Flying High Not in Denisonian's [Bobbie Lightfoot] Wildest Dream," Oct. 11, 1987.

"Former Resident [Billy Medlin Galef] To Be Neighbor with Reagans," May 3, 1987.

"Frank Colbert Not Only Colbert With a Ferry," June 14, 1987.

"Handicap No Obstacle for Former Denisonian [Diane Fields DeVries]," July 5, 1987.

"Herald May Soon Pass the White Glove Test," Sept. 13, 1987.

"Historic [Denison High] School Could Get Second Chance," Sept. 6, 1987.

"Home Is Where the Heart Is—Denison," Aug. 2, 1987. Denison reunion in California.

"It's Business as Usual Despite Pending Sale [of *Denison Herald*]," Oct. 18, 1987.

"Katy's 75th Anniversary Halted by President's Death," Mar. 15, 1987.

"Latest Hall of Famer [Billy Holcomb] Deserves the Honor," Nov. 22, 1987.

"Looking Ahead: Panel To Study Needs of Community for Next 20 Years," Nov. 15, 1987.

"Main Street Project Often Success Story," Dec. 13, 1987.

"Not Every Drug Store Has Its Own Animals, but Kingston's 'Has It'," Jan. 11, 1987.

"Pending Sale [of *Denison Herald*] Triggers No Immediate Changes," Nov. 29, 1987.

"Plans for Denison's Future Will Unfold in '88," Dec. 27, 1987.

"Reporters Wish for the 'Good Old Days'," July 12, 1987.

"Retirement Party Honors [Richard] Riggins," Mar. 25, 1987.

"St. Xavier Nuns Being Displaced in Fort Worth," June 21, 1987.

"Staying on Right Track Not Always Simple," Jan. 25, 1987.

"Tennessee Roots Lead to Revolutionary Ancestor," June 7, 1987.

"The Answer Is ... History; Denison: Tracking the History of a Railroad Town," July 30, 1987.

"The Gang's All Here, and It's Ready to Roll," Nov. 22, 1987. Motorcycle riders.

"Well-Known Educator, Doctor, Lawyer, Got Their Start in Denison," Aug. 16, 1987. Linus Wright, Claude Organ, Frank Finn.

"Writing Autobiography Displays Real Spunk," Nov. 1, 1987.

"Zoo Time in Gainesville," Aug. 2, 1987. Frank Buck Zoo.

1988

"15-Year-Old Documented Day President [John F. Kennedy] Shot," Dec. 4, 1988.

"1888—The Good Old Days in Denison," Oct. 2, 1988.

"1913 Denison Recalled in Early Day Photo," July 24, 1988.

"1938 South Gale Grads Stayed Close to Home," Mar. 20, 1988.

"An Editorial: Life Goes On," Aug. 12, 1988. Merger of MKT and Union Pacific railroads.

"Book of Texas Bests [by Kirk Dooley] Outbrags Best Braggers," Oct. 16, 1988.

"Cabiness Optimistic About Denison's Future" (Priorities for Denison, part 7), May 22, 1988.

"Childbirth Is Not What It Used To Be," Jan. 3, 1988.

"Community Plan Applauded as Blueprint for the Future," Aug. 3, 1988.

"Denison Ambassador [C.J. McManus] Passes Away," Feb. 4, 1988.

"Denison Area Looks Different from a Balloon," Oct. 9, 1988.

"Denison Bears Name of Presidential Candidate [George Denison]," May 1, 1988.

"Denison Man [Bobby Eugene McDade] Shot To Death," Apr. 25, 1988.

"Denison to Portugal—A Small World After All," June 26, 1988.

"Denison's 'Good Old Days' Are Eye-Openers," Oct. 30, 1988.

"Denison's History Has Many Local Followers," Sept. 11, 1988.

"Donrey Media Group Officially Buys Herald," Mar. 6, 1988.

"Early Rail System Transported Residents," Feb. 7, 1988.

"Election Fanfare Put to Rest Until '92," Nov. 13, 1988.

"Familiar Problems Date Back to 1860," Aug. 14, 1988.

"Former Denisonian [A.W. Roberson] Works for Equal Rights," Aug. 28, 1988.

"Former Denisonian [Mary Sullenberger] Has the Best Job There Is," May 29, 1988.

"Graduates in Year 2000 Look at Denison," May 22, 1988.

"Group Sees Need to Emphasize Positive Side of Denison School System" (Priorities for Denison, part 3), May 17, 1988.

"Group Sees Need to Push Tourism" (Priorities for Denison, part 5), May 19, 1988.

"Herald Records Go 'Down Memory Lane'," Sept. 25, 1988.

"Herald Senior Newsman [John Clift] Marks 40th Year," Apr. 10, 1988.

"Immediate and Long-Range Goals Call for Improving Downtown Area" (Priorities for Denison, part 4), May 18, 1988.

"Industrial Development Team Ready to Intensify Its Efforts" (Priorities for Denison, part 6), May 20, 1988.

"Industry Recruitment Top Need for City: Group Lists City's Goals," Apr. 24, 1988.

"Infrastructure a Community Planning Priority" (Priorities for Denison, part 2), May 16, 1988.

"Is Denison Taking Steps in the Right Direction?" Jan. 31, 1988.

"It's Decision Time Across Country," Nov. 6, 1988.

"June '89 Scenario Not Necessarily a Spoof," Feb. 21, 1988.

"Life Takes New Turn for Pottsboro Osteopath [Dr. Clinton Burns]," Apr. 10, 1988.

"Mail, Magazines Give Varied Column Ideas," Jan. 17, 1988.

"Memories of Home Spur Denison Reunion [in California]," July 31, 1988.

"Newsman [Byron B. Buzbee] Writes Final '30' to Long Career" (obituary), Aug. 7, 1988.

"Political Parties Get Better With Age," Aug. 21, 1988. 1952 and 1956.

"Retired Teacher [Verna McClure McDonald] Writing on Raynal [Elementary School] Classes," June 5, 1988.

"Returning to Two-Way Traffic Along Texas 75-A Touted" (Priorities for Denison, part 1), May 15, 1988.

"Scouts Begin Holiday Season Helping Others," Nov. 27, 1988.

"Stop Everything! The President's Been Shot!" Nov. 20, 1988. John F. Kennedy.

"Task Forces Attempting to Establish Denison's Needs," Jan. 24, 1988.

"Texomaland No Longer Just Around the Lake," Feb. 28, 1988.

"The Answer Is ... History: Development of Denison Tied to Railroad Business," July 31, 1988.

"Thousands Invested in Their Future While Students at DHS," Nov. 20, 1988.

"Viaduct Not What It Once Was—Thank Goodness," Sept. 4, 1988.

"Weight Loss Changes Woman's [Lynda Kerley] Life, Not Just Her Body," Sept. 18, 1988.

"Youth Center Deserves Serious Consideration," June 12, 1988.

1989

"100 Years of Newspapering Has Interesting Sidelights," July 23, 1989.

"1943 Letter Tells of WWII Worries," Feb. 5, 1989.

"1980's Filled with Headline-Grabbing Events," Dec. 31, 1989.

"All-Pro [Vernon Holland] Going All Out for Area Youngsters," Oct. 15, 1989.

"CCC Boys To Gather for Reunion in Dallas," Sept. 10, 1989.

"Changing Times: Clickety Clack to Beep Beep," July 23, 1989.

"City Falls Short of Predicted 1990 Population," Feb. 12, 1989.

"Clean Roadways Important to One Denison Area Man [B.K. Francis]," Nov. 28, 1989.

"Denison Landmark [MKT Depot] Celebrates 80 Years," Oct. 29, 1989.

"Denison Loses a Champion [Jerry Crenshaw]" (obituary), Oct. 6, 1989.

"Denison Night in Omaha," Aug. 27, 1989.

"Denisonian [Ed Abshire] Recalls Early-Day Baseball," Apr. 2, 1989.

"Double: [Lt. Michael] Mahan Flies High in New Movie," Nov. 15, 1989.

"Extra Proclaimed Martial Law in 1922," July 30, 1989.

"Famous Son [Dwight D. Eisenhower] Recognized as Year 100 Nears," Feb. 19, 1989.

"Former Herald Reporter [Terry Leonard] Has Interesting AP Assignment," Jan. 29, 1989.

"[Franklin D.] Roosevelt's Visit to Denison Draws 25,000 Persons," June 18, 1989.

"GCC Photography Teacher [Kathryn Allen] Retiring," Apr. 30, 1989.

"Herald Ace Reporter [Irene Flaherty] Hangs Up Her Camera," Nov. 5, 1989.

"Jukebox Music's Still In — It Just Costs More," Nov. 19, 1989.

"Law Enforcement Wins Out Over Killer, Mob," May 7, 1989. John C. Carlton pursues John Hogan, Nov. 1887.

"Lewises Get Surprise at DHS Class Reunion," May 29, 1989.

"Lots Sold 117 Years Ago for Denison," Sept. 24, 1989.

"MKT, UP Retiree [Mike McNellis] Making Denison Home," Aug. 20, 1989.

"Needed: Volunteers and Participants for Oct. 14 Events," Oct. 8, 1989.

"Never Know Where You'll Find Denisonians," Aug. 20, 1989. Bettie Vincent.

"Old Hotel [First Denison Hotel] Went Out in a Blaze of Glory," Feb. 26, 1989. 500 W. Main St.

"[Olivia] Barton Compiles Book on Blue Grads," May 28, 1989.

"Photographs Are Important Part of Our Roots," Jan. 15, 1989.

"Recipes Could Produce Interesting Results," Jan. 8, 1989.

"School 'Annual' Produced by '44 [DHS] Class," Nov. 26, 1989. Reunions.

"[Sherman-Denison] Twins Took Championship 40 Years Ago," Mar. 26, 1989.

"Street Walkers Find Hidden Treasures," June 11, 1989. Downtown Denison.

"Tabloid [May 23, 1939] Saluted DHS Graduates 50 Years Ago," Mar. 19, 1989.

"The Answer Is ... History: Denison's Railroad Roots Run Deep; Site of Railhead Kept Secret Until All Deals Closed in Sept. 1872," July 30, 1989.

"Vin Fiz Pilot Honored in SAC Museum," Aug. 27, 1989.

"Washington-Bound Stingerettes Follow in DHS Footsteps," Jan. 22, 1989.

"XXI [Club] To Join 100-Year Circle in 1990," Oct. 22, 1989.

1990

"25 Years Later Ike's Namesake [Dwight David Gaines] Returns for Visit," July 2, 1990.

"200 Flags Could Greet Birthplace Visitors," July 22, 1990.

"All Around Denison," Oct. 23, 1990. DHS class reunions.

"All Around Denison," Oct. 7, 1990. Eisenhower born in Denison.

"Barbering Trade Goes Way Back," Apr. 15, 1990.

"[Charles] Johnson Last Grandchild of Spy Captain," Oct. 7, 1990.

"Denison Temperatures Hit Record Low in 1899," Jan. 21, 1990.

"Denison-Bells Rails Laid in City's First Year," Feb. 25, 1990.

"Denison's Cruisin' Club Hosting Local Version of 'Bandstand'," Mar. 11, 1990.

"Denisonian Related Story of Mine Disaster," Apr. 22, 1990.

"Denisonians-Texans Celebrate Independence," Mar. 4, 1990.

"Eisenhower a Household Word in Denison," May 20, 1990.

"[Eisenhower] Birthplace Address Questioned, Documented," Oct. 21, 1990.

"Fame Comes to Tahoe and Red River Boats," Oct. 28, 1990. *Annie P.*

"First Brick Streets Didn't Go Down Smoothly," July 29, 1990.

"Flood Waters Raging Throughout Texoma," May 3, 1990.

"Former Employees To Recall Memories of [Cotton] Mill," Sept. 16, 1990.

"Former Resident [James L. Pattillo] Surfaces in Magazine," Nov. 4, 1990.

"[Grayson County Frontier] Village Dedicates Museum," June 4, 1990.

"Historical Answers: Denison Is a Child of the Katy Railroad," July 29, 1990.

"'Ike' Mania Hits Former, Present Residents," July 8, 1990.

"Ike's Birthplace Area To Double in Size," Oct. 1, 1990.

"Ike's Sister-in-Law [Lucy Eisenhower] Visits Birthplace," June 20, 1990.

"[Judge R.C.] Vaughan Honored by Bar," June 8, 1990.

"[Kenneth E.] Kinnamon Had His Eye on Baseball," Mar. 4, 1990.

"Local Writer's [Sherrie McLeRoy] Book Captures Sophia's [Porter] Story," July 1, 1990.

"Memories of Yules Past Are Heartwarming," Dec. 23, 1990.

"Mother's Day—A Time of Joy and Sadness," May 13, 1990.

"Old Book Salutes World War II Men, Women," Sept. 2, 1990.

"Oval Office Ceremony Takes Kochs to Capital," Dec. 30, 1990.

"Picture [Hanna Drug Store] Looked Familiar Because It Was," Nov. 25, 1990.

"Postcards Tell a Story of Early Denison," Nov. 18, 1990.

"Regardless, She [Martha Douglas] Will Stay [at Lake Texoma]," May 3, 1990.

"Stern: Quedlinburg [Germany] Seeking Funds," June 21, 1990.

"Teacher [James R. Parrish] Publishes Ideas on Crime [and] Prisons," Jan. 14, 1990. Mayor Flem Coleman.

"Terrell [School] Students Built Ike's Picket Fence," Aug. 19, 1990.

"Texoma's Ready To Save a Little Rain for Later," May 6, 1990.

"Thurber Bricks Paved Denison in Early Days," Aug. 5, 1990.

"U.S. Flag Symbol of Freedom in America," June 24, 1990.

"White Pig Was the Place Kids Got Together," Dec. 2, 1990.

1991

"1878 UFO Sighting Near City Told in Story," Feb. 17, 1991.

"Book [*Katy's Baby*] Renews Interest in Denison's Past," June 30, 1991.

"Burial Records List [B.M.] Steele and [Lawrence] Washington," July 21, 1991.

"Cheers and Tears of Joy Begin," Mar. 3, 1991. Desert Storm troops return.

"Denison Man [Claude Arthur] Among First Picked in 1940," Jan. 13, 1991.

"Digging Up Denison's History," May 5, 1991. Bill Snell.

"Dr. [Lawrence] Washington No Stranger to Herald Pages," July 7, 1991.

"Former [Perrin Air Force] Base Still Viable Part of Community," June 30, 1991.

"Hollywood Was [Melvin] Bryant's Life," July 14, 1991.

"Lions Hear of Plans for Book [*Katy's Baby*, by Jack Maguire] on Denison's History," June 20, 1991.

"Maguire Book [*Katy's Baby*] Goes to Printer," Nov. 14, 1991.

"Markers Came From Under Our Noses," June 16, 1991. Sherman TX.

"[McDougall] Hotel Room Tags Inspire Search for History," Feb. 24, 1991.

"Memorabilia Belongs Where Intended," June 9, 1991. Mary Heck's diploma.

"Newspaper Tells of World War I Happenings," Jan. 27, 1991.

"'Old Cowboy' [B.K. Francis] Polices County Roads," Apr. 21, 1991.

"Pre-1940 Living an Education for Youngsters," Aug. 11, 1991.

"Reunion Takes Denison to California," Aug. 11, 1991.

"Six-Year-Old [Robert Epperson] Would Rather Draw Than Study," May 12, 1991.

"Tombstone Mystery Tells of Assassination [of B.M. Steele]," July 14, 1991.

"[Vernon] Beckham's Roots Run Deep in Denison," Apr. 28, 1991.

1992

"Bed Race Creates Pre-Event Shenanigans," July 5, 1992. 4th of July.

"Bid Will Be Offered [by Cynthia Mabary Hayes] for McDaniel School," May 17, 1992.

"Car Salesman [Gary Dunlap] Entombed in Ice," Apr. 3, 1992.

"City Had Texas' First Hard-Surface Roads," Aug. 23, 1992.

"Could Citizens Operate Ike's Birthplace?" Aug. 2, 1992.

"[D.D.] McKnight Banquet Speaker for NAACP," Apr. 29, 1992.

"Denison First in KTB [Keep Texas Beautiful] Contest," June 4, 1992.

"Denison Receives [Keep Texas Beautiful] Award," July 12, 1992.

"Denison Second Home to [Robert J.] Eaton," Mar. 17, 1992. CEO, Chrysler Corporation.

"'Estelline' Author [Jane Roberts Wood] Returns to Sherman," Feb. 2,

1992.

"Favorite Quotations Benefitted [Houston Elementary] School," Nov. 29, 1992.

"Grant 'Took' Denison After Taking Richmond," Apr. 19, 1992. [First U.S. president to set foot in Texas while in office.]

"Grayson One of Four [Texas] Counties for [Ross] Perot," Nov. 8, 1992.

"Hammering Out a Life: Retired Bells Carpenter [J.T. Thomas] Still an Early Riser," Jan. 19, 1992.

"Help Sought in Solving 'Brakie' Mystery," Jan. 5, 1992.

"He's Another Sort of Father ... [Fred] Caldwell's Special 'Children'," June 21, 1992.

"'Infant Wonder' [Denison] To Mark 120th Birthday," Sept. 20, 1992. Highlights of Denison history.

"[Joseph G.] McCoy's Historical Marker Area Gets Facelift," Mar. 1, 1992.

"Katy Railroad Repaired Underpasses in '48," Jan. 26, 1992.

"New [Texas] Tourist Center Is Funded," Feb. 26, 1992.

"No Room in the ... Graveyard," Feb. 6, 1992. Oakwood Cemetery.

"Nov. 22, 1963, Began as a Normal Workday," Nov. 22, 1992. Kennedy Assassination.

"Presidential Campaign Picks Up Local Speed," Apr. 12, 1992.

"Red River Railroad Museum Contains History: Memorabilia Being Added Daily," Feb. 23, 1992.

"Steam [Railroad] Engine Brings Back Memories of Bygone Era," Aug. 23, 1992.

"Summer Reunions Are Good for the Soul," July 12, 1992.

"Thaddeus Fowler Drew Towns, Not Trains," Feb. 23, 1992. Bird's-eye maps.

"The South Could rise Again—In Denison," June 7, 1992. Sons of the Confederacy.

"Thousands Attend 'Quiet' Denison Wedding [at Diamond Jubilee, 1947]," Sept. 6, 1992.

"Top Stars [Reba McEntire, Dolly Parton, Brooks & Dunn] Shine Brightly in Denison," May 31, 1992.

"Two Local Banking Pioneers [Laura Jacobs, Doris Jones] Are Retiring Next Month," Dec. 20, 1992.

"Veterans Reunite in Denison," May 24, 1992. 1920th Quartermaster Truck Company.

"Yule Lights Add Sparkle to Downtown Area," Dec. 6, 1992.

1993

"120-Year-Old Spike-Laying Not a Secret Now," Mar. 14, 1993.

"BPW [Business and Professional Women's Club] Kicks Off National Week with 'Salute to Industry'," Oct. 19, 1993.

"Declaration of Friendship Inked Between Cognac-City," Oct. 25, 1993.

"Denison Dam's 50th Birthday Draws More Attention Than Its Dedication," Oct. 22, 1993.

"Donations [by Robert C. Stevens] Outline City's Start," May 16, 1993.

"Former Denisonian [John Bengel] Heading Urban Corps," Jan. 31, 1993.

"Grand Exalted Ruler [Charles F. Williams] Visits Denison Elks," Dec. 8, 1993.

"Huge Crowd Greets [Memorial Day] Parade," June 1, 1993.

"[James E. "Jim"] Nugent, [Jack] Maguire Set for [Golden] Spike Ceremony," Mar. 9, 1993.

"[Liz] Carpenter Salutes Seniors," Feb. 19, 1993.

"[Liz] Carpenter's Sense of Humor a Real Delight," Feb. 21, 1993.

1994

"Denison, Abilene Have Something in Common ... 'We Like Ike'," Oct. 9, 1994.

[NOTE: Donna Hord Hunt resigned from *The Denison Herald*, March 1994]

1995

"Man Who Helped 'Create' Denison Enjoys Retirement," Sept. 12, 1995. C.J. McManus.

Tribute to John Clift, in "Feature: John Clift, 1916–1995," Jan. 29, 1995.

1996

"Merger [of *The Denison Herald* and *Sherman Democrat*] Spotlights Change," Aug. 30, 1996.

Denison Post

2000

"Celebrants Turn Out to Honor Eisenhower's 110th Birthday," Oct. 19, 2000.

"Denison's War Kids Recall Pearl Harbor," Dec. 7, 2000.

"DHI [Denison Heritage Inc.] Shifts Plans for Old School to Phases," Nov. 30, 2000.

"Offspring of Local Tree to Stand Silent Vigil," Dec. 14, 2000.

"Perspective: 'Chicken Night' at the Embers Was a Special Treat in Denison," Sept. 14, 2000.

"Perspective: As a Photographer, the History Is in Identifying the Picture," Nov. 9, 2000.

"Perspective: Days of Denison's Interurban Making a Comeback in the Area," Aug. 31, 2000.

"Perspective: Denison Was Always Special to Hometown Writer Jack Maguire," Sept. 7, 2000.

"Perspective: Fair Park's Women's Museum Does Female Pioneers Justice," Oct. 26, 2000.

"Perspective: Hotel Denison Is a Reminder That Past and Present Are One," Aug. 3, 2000.

"Perspective: Johnny Goldston's Patriotism, Spirit Still Thrive in Denison," July 4, 2000.

"Perspective: Mamie the Cat Is Missing, and [Eisenhower] Birthplace Staff Wants Her Back," Sept. 28, 2000.

"Perspective: Pearl Harbor Day 2000 Will Help Mark Denison's Place in History," Dec. 7, 2000.

"Perspective: Retirement Provides [Donna Hunt] a Chance To Get Back to Newspapering," June 29, 2000.

"Perspective: Santa Claus? You Bet He's Real, and Alive and Well in Denison!" Dec. 21, 2000.

"Perspective: Years of California Reunions Helped Denisonians 'Go Home'," Oct. 5, 2000.

2001

"1872 Was a Denison Christmas to Remember," Dec. 23, 2001.

"Area Camp Fire Pioneer [Teresa Vehle Wegener] to Celebrate Her 90th Birthday," Dec. 6, 2001.

"Artist [Mike Williams] Takes Up the Cause of Helping Support, Promote Downtown Denison," Sept. 19, 2001.

"Before There Was Denison, a Tent Settlement Called Red River City Sprang Up to Herald the Railroad," June 3, 2001.

"Bell Is a Focal Point of Old [Denison High] School," Sept. 17, 2001.

"Camp Fire Girl [Teresa Vehle Wegener] Reaches Age 90," Dec. 9, 2001.

"Denison and the 'Bridge War'," Nov. 14, 2001.

"[Dr. Dorothy] Rushing Provides Glimpse of Texana at Thursday Review Club Meeting," Apr. 26, 2001.

"[Eisenhower] Birthplace Is Ready for Ike's 111th [Birthday]," Oct. 8, 2001.

"Emblems of Texas: Bluebonnet," June 12, 2001.

"Emblems of Texas: Confederate Air Force," Sept. 11, 2001.

"Emblems of Texas: Crape Myrtle's Distinction Is Well-Deserved," July 5, 2001.

"Emblems of Texas: Denison's Cotton Mill Holds Important Place in Annals of Texas History," Aug. 14, 2001.

"Emblems of Texas: 'Friendship' Is the Ideal Word Used to Describe Texans," Sept. 19, 2001.

"Emblems of Texas: Guadalupe Bass," Aug. 21, 2001.

"Emblems of Texas: Lone Star Flag," Aug. 28, 2001.

"Emblems of Texas: Longhorn, Armadillo Stake Their Claim to Fame in Texas," Aug. 7, 2001.

"Emblems of Texas: Mockingbird," June 4, 2001. First of "Emblems of Texas" series.

"Emblems of Texas: Nothing on the Dinner Table Says Texas Like Chili," Sept. 25, 2001.

"Emblems of Texas: Of Peppers and Plants," Oct. 10, 2001.

"Emblems of Texas: Texas Has a Place in Pre-history, Too," July 12, 2001.

"Emblems of Texas: Texas Pecans," June 25, 2001.

"Emblems of Texas: Texas' Own Flying Mammal and Musical Instrument Really Are Official Symbols," Oct. 17, 2001.

"Emblems of Texas: The Exploits of *USS Texas* Won Honor for Her, State," Oct. 2, 2001.

"Fred Bulloch Was a Call Boy on the MKT," July 12, 2001. [NOTE: Title may not be exact.]

"Harry Gaines and Sugar Bottom," Aug. 27, 2001. [NOTE: Title may not be exact.]

"Heroes Are Everywhere," Sept. 16, 2001. World Trade Center disaster.

"Historic Sight: Fairview Cemetery Holds a Special Place in Local History," June 12, 2001.

"Jim 'Lucky Jim' Holland" (obituary), Oct. 31, 2001.

114

"John F. Kennedy Assassination," Nov. 12, 2001. [NOTE: Title may not be exact.]

"Local Ceremony Honors Eisenhower," Oct. 15, 2001.

"Marcia Ball Re-Opens Renovated Kidd-Key Auditorium: A Review," Nov. 11, 2001. [NOTE: Title and date may not be exact.]

"Martha 'Queenie' Simms" (obituary), Aug. 16, 2001. Old Ironsides.

"'Night of Terror' Murders Here Never Officially Solved" (part 3), July 12, 2001.

"Night of Terror One of the Darkest in Denison History" (part 1), June 17, 2001.

"Perspective: A Beautiful Start To a Terrible Day [11 Sept. 2001]," Sept. 13, 2001.

"Perspective: A Denison Connection with the *USS Texas*," Oct. 14 or 24, 2001. Adm. Adolphus Andrews, Berenice Platter Andrews.

"Perspective: A Jewel of a Texas Lady" [Lady Bird Johnson], Dec. 19, 2001.

"Perspective: A Local George Washington Connection" (part 1), Dec. 2, 2001.

"Perspective: A Taste of [Union Pacific Railroad's] Challenger" (part 2), Oct. 29, 2001.

"Perspective: As Denison Grew, More Names Emerged for City's Streets" (part 2), May 17, 2001.

"Perspective: Carpenter's Bluff Bridge Is a Vital, Historical Link on the Red [River]," Jan. 18, 2001.

"Perspective: Denison's Street Names Lean Heavily Toward the Railroad" (part 1), May 10, 2001.

"Perspective: Denison's West End Was a Lively Place" (part 2), Sept. 30, 2001.

"Perspective: Denison's West End Was a Thriving Area" (part 1), Sept. 23, 2001.

"Perspective: Drugstore Reminiscences Spark Memories of Other Early Sites" (part 2), Feb. 22, 2001. Harris Drug.

"Perspective: Genealogical Quests Have Gotten a Friendly Boost from Technology," Aug. 23, 2001.

"Perspective: Growing Up in a Drug Store" (part 1), Feb. 15, 2001. Loi-Mac Pharmacy.

"Perspective: Historical Marker for Dr. Lawrence A. Washington" (part 2), Dec. 6, 2001. [NOTE: Title and date may not be exact.]

"Perspective: In New Book, Late Denisonian's [Jack Maguire] Love of Texas Is Most Evident," Apr. 26, 2001. *Texas Originals: Peons, Plain People and Presidents.*

"Perspective: Memories of Growing Up on the Red River," June 14, 2001.

"Perspective: Message in a Vase Holds Special Place in Author's Heart," June 28, 2001.

"Perspective: MKT Depot, Denison's Arch," Aug. 12, 2001. C.J. McManus.

"Perspective: Notorious 'Doc' Holliday May Once Have Called Denison Home," Feb. 8, 2001.

"Perspective: Reprise—The West End Story Just Keeps Growing" (part 3), Oct. 7, 2001.

"Perspective: Son of Slain Denison Man [Bobby Lee Spencer] Still Has Fond Memories of the Town," Mar. 8, 2001.

"Perspective: Texas Theater Sign Finds an Appropriate New Home," July 19, 2001.

"Perspective: Thankfully, This July 4 Not Like the One in 1879," July 8, 2001.

"Perspective: Wisconsin Relative Curious about Denison's Jacobs' Hotel," Mar. 1, 2001.

"Red River Currents: Butterfield Stage Put Denison Area on Route to California," Aug. 19, 2001.

"Red River Currents: Butterfield Stage Stops Can Still Be Pinpointed in Area," Aug. 5, 2001.

"Red River Currents: Denison of the Past Provides Rich Memories for Some Folks," Sept. 2, 2001. Eleven separate items.

"Red River Currents: Denison POW Camp an Interesting Story," Sept. 9, 2001.

"Red River Currents: Oral History Is Still a Key to Site of Red River City," July 22, 2001.

"Red River Currents: 'Red' Hall Started the Denison Clean-up," Aug. 26, 2001.

"Red River Currents: Search for Red River City Location Sparks Reply from Resident," June 10, 2001.

"Red River Currents: Trash Dump Helps Pinpoint Location of Red River City," July 29, 2001.

"Red River Currents: Writings, Photo [of Red River City] Reveal Much of Denison's Past," July 15, 2001.

"Remembering the Day President Kennedy Was Shot," Nov. 20, 2001.

"Ronnie D. Arthur" (obituary), Apr. 5, 2001. [NOTE: Actual title unknown.]

"Silent Witness: [D-Day] Tree Will Be Dedicated June 6," June 4, 2001.

"Sister of Denison Woman Escapes [World Trade Center] Tower Before Crash," Sept. 13, 2001.

"Smith Wood Preserving Company Was at One Time a Boon for Denison," Sept. 10, 2001.

"Students Learn History at Fairview Cemetery," Sept. 20, 2001.

"The Plot Thickens in the Tale of 'Denison's Night of Terror' in '92" (part 2), June 24, 2001.

"Three Cheers for the Green Stamps Folks," Nov. 29, 2001.

"Tomb Rater: Denison Man [Michael Cross] Gathers Data for Texas Tombstone Project," June 22, 2001.

"Train Stop [Union Pacific's Challenger] Gives Many the Thrill of a Lifetime" (part 2), Oct. 31, 2001.

"Tree-Planting [D-Day] Ceremony Honors Veterans," June 7, 2001.

2002

"Denison and the Butterfield Stage" (part 3), Feb. 19, 2002. Red River to Sand Springs.

"Denison Musicians Are Honored at Prairie View," Apr. 1, 2002.

"Eisenhower's Granddaughter [Susan Eisenhower] Speaks in Denison," Sept. 30, 2002.

"Hometown Boy [Aubrey Webb] Makes Good," Mar. 22, 2002.

"[Joanna] Clark Recounts Life of Pioneer [Sophia Suttonfield Aughinbaugh Coffee Butt Porter]" (part 1), Mar. 22, 2002.

"Perspective: A Doughboy's [Joe Newcomb] Story" (part 1), Jan. 14, 2002. 27th Ambulance Corps in World War I.

"Perspective: A [Denison Public] Library Treasure," Nov. 29, 2002. Dixie Brewer Foster.

"Perspective: A Name in the Music World [Goebel Reeves]," Aug. 13, 2002.

"Perspective: A Survivor's [C.M. Eldredge] Tale," Aug. 9, 2002. Sinking of the Sultana.

"Perspective: Ambrose [TX] Discoveries," June 30, 2002. Bebe Bodamer, Paul Jennings.

"Perspective: Anvils and Cannon Fire," July 16, 2002. Fourth of July noise.

"Perspective: Back to Colbert [Oklahoma]" (part 2), Mar. 16, 2002.

"Perspective: Back to the Doughboys" (part 2), Jan. 23, 2002. Joe Newcomb, World War I.

"Perspective: Brogdon Cemetery" (Brogdon Springs, part 3) Jan. 31, 2002.

"Perspective: Brogdon Springs Still Flowing" (part 2), Jan. 24, 2002.

"Perspective: Cherry Dairy Holds Memories," Sept. 13, 2002.

"Perspective: Church [Messenger's Chapel United Methodist] Gets New Home," Sept. 9, 2002.

"Perspective: Clash of Ideals," May 23, 2002. Lee-Peacock feud.

"Perspective: Colbert [OK] Recollections" (part 1), Mar. 6, 2002.

"Perspective: Denison and Sophia [Suttonfield Aughinbaugh Coffee Butt Porter]" (part 2), Mar. 31, 2002.

"Perspective: Denisonians Are Just About Everywhere," June 3, 2002. Tommy Loy.

"Perspective: Donna Hunt: Park Ranger," Aug. 7, 2002.

"Perspective: Earlier Crash [Empire State Building, 1945] Was Also a Shocker," Jan. 13, 2002.

"Perspective: Exhibit Spotlights Rail Transportation," Nov. 11, 2002.

"Perspective: Forgotten Treasures," Aug. 21, 2002. Dee Gaines.

"Perspective: Good Old July 4 [1876]," July 3, 2002.

"Perspective: Hooking Up the Horses," Nov. 26, 2002. Beatrice Weaver, covered wagon trip in 1934.

"Perspective: It's Nice to Have a Refuge," Jan. 3, 2002. Hagerman Wildlife Refuge.

"Perspective: Joining Together Again," Oct. 22, 2002. DHS Class of 1953 reunion.

"Perspective: Pillsbury Meant a Lot to the Community," Dec. 8, 2002.

"Perspective: Presidents Visited County with Grandeur," Nov. 4, 2002.

"Perspective: [Railroad] Chapel Cars Once Stopped in Denison," Dec. 14, 2002.

"Perspective: Recalling Sugar Bottom" (part 1), Aug. 23, 2002. Harry Gaines.

"Perspective: Remembering Gene Autry," Feb. 21, 2002. Howard McCarley, Pat Watson.

"Perspective: Ruth Ann Overbeck," Jan. 6, 2002. [NOTE: Title may not be exact.]

"Perspective: Sugar Bottom Firemen," Aug. 29, 2002. Fire Department history.

"Perspective: Sugar Bottom Shenanigans" (part 2), Aug. 25, 2002.

"Perspective: The Ghost Patrol" (Colbert OK stories, part 3), Mar. 21, 2002.

"Perspective: The Piano Lessons," June 14, 2002. Bebe Bodamer.

"Perspective: The Things You Learn," July 28, 2002. Claud Easterly's taped memories.

"Perspective: There's Mystery Behind the Artwork," Dec. 17, 2002. Boxcar art.

"Perspective: Unwelcome Press," Jan. 21, 2002. Rosemary Clooney, Jose Ferrer.

"Perspective: Water, Water Everywhere" (Brogdon Springs, part 1), Jan. 15, 2002.

"Perspective: When FDR Came to Town [13 June 1936], Denison Turned Out," Jan. 7, 2002.

"Perspective: Win a Few, Lose a Few," Feb. 17, 2002. Red River ferries, Railroad Strike of 1922.

"Pink Hill" (part 1), Apr. 24, 2002. [NOTE: Title and date may not be exact.]

"Pink Hill" (part 2), Apr. 26, 2002. [NOTE: Title and date may not be exact.]

"Rumbleys Explain the History of Ragtime Music in America," Mar. 22, 2002.

"Ruth Pierce, Artist," July 8, 2002. [NOTE: Title and date may not be exact.]

"St. Xavier's Building Gone But Not Forgotten," May 13, 2002. St. Xavier's reunion.

"The Next Stop Along the [Butterfield Overland Mail] Trail" (part 2), Feb. 12, 2002. Red River to Sand Springs.

"Tommy Loy, Former Cowboys Trumpeter, Dies at 72," Oct. 18, 2002.

"Tracing the Butterfield Overland Mail Stagecoach" (part 1), Feb. 5, 2002. Red River to Sand Springs.

"Train Robbery on the Katy [24 Aug. 1921]," Nov. 7, 2002. [NOTE: Title may not be exact.]

"Unveiling the Story Behind the Eisenhower Sculpture," Apr. 2, 2002. Sculptor Electra Waggoner.

"Woodlake a Wonderful Spot for Early Memories," Mar. 5, 2002.

2003

"Perspective: Denison Man [Ben J. Wells] Involved in Space Program," Feb. 10, 2003.

"Perspective: Most of Us Never Forget Our Roots," Jan. 27, 2003. Circus tragedy, Liberty Bell, naming Dad and Lad's, Citizens National Bank gets air conditioning, Centennial Plate, Texas stone marker, DHS Class of 1925 reunions, Claud Easterly.

"Perspective: Others Recall Powerful Storm [1949]," Jan. 31, 2003.

"Perspective: Recalling the Ice Storm of 1945," Jan. 28, 2003.

"Perspective: Record Provides Grist for the Mill," Jan. 15, 2003. Grist mill, T.R. Williams, C.B. Sullenberger.

"Perspective: [Red River Wagon] Bridge Was Part of Denison History," Feb. 21, 2003.

"Perspective: Remembering Willie and Joe" (part 1), Feb. 17, 2003. Cartoonist Bill Mauldin.

"Perspective: Soapbox, and a Story of the Eisenhower Birthplace [Gruenlds of Oberammergau]," Feb. 4, 2003. Grist mill.

"Perspective: The Rest of the Story" (part 2), Feb. 24, 2003. Cartoonist Bill Mauldin, Bob Elston, Dr. Aaron Dry, Rayson Billey, ""Willie."

Unknown Date

"Billy Holcomb and Gene Autry," date unknown. [NOTE: Title not exact.]

"Dwight D. Eisenhower Museum in Oberammergau, Germany," published "not long" before Feb. 3, 2003. Elisabeth and Claus Gruendl. [NOTE: Title not exact.]

"Memories of 1940s, 1950s, 1960s," date unknown. [NOTE: Title not exact.]

"Noel Wall Tells of Oklahoma City Bombing," probably 2001. [NOTE: Title not exact.]

[NOTE: Donna Hord Hunt left the *Denison Daily Post* in February 2003 and began writing a column for the *Herald Democrat* on Mar. 16, 2003. According to Dwayne Wilder, the last issue of the *Denison Post* was published on Sept. 15, 2003.]

Herald Democrat

2003

"1921 Home To Cook for Thrasher Crews Donated to Frontier Village," Mar. 25, 2003.

"A Colorful Foundation" ("Characters," part 2), Aug. 20, 2003. Dr. Alexander W. Acheson.

"A Common Thread of Yesterday's Texoma," Nov. 30, 2003. Scholl and Maughs family, Central Ward School, Merry Maud Farm, Tropical Gardens Nightclub, George Knaur, chickens.

"Alumni Group [Denison Alumni Association] Ready to Grow," Sept. 24, 2003.

"An Amazing Choctaw Indian [Rayson Billey]," Mar. 28, 2003. World War II, Bob Elston, Dr. Aaron Dry, cartoonist Bill Mauldin.

"Ashburn's [Ice Cream] 'The Best Yet'," June 11, 2003.

"By George! Denison Has a Tie to More Than One [U.S.] President," July 3, 2003. Dr. Lawrence A. Washington.

"Church [Messenger's Chapel UMC] Makes a Holy Trip," June 8, 2003.

"Coontown [AKA Caney] Cemetery Rises Like a Phoenix," May 11, 2003. Near Savoy TX.

"Cream of the Crop [Ashburn's Creamery]," May 22, 2003.

"Crossing Paths in Denison, Texas," Oct. 29, 2003. J.F. Probst, Maj. A.B. Ostrander, Rowdy Joe Lowe.

"[Dee] Gaines Lived His Dream, and That's No Bull," June 4, 2003. Bullfighting.

"Denison Celebrates Its 131st Birthday ... on Christmas," Dec. 10, 2003. First train.

"Denison Had Run of the Mills," Dec. 31, 2003. Flour, cotton, canning, hosiery, refrigerator cars.

"Denison Woman [Louise Lane Heath] Recalls Letter from Dr. [Alexander W.] Acheson," Nov. 2, 2003.

"Denison's Early Days Could Rival the Old Western Movie," Mar. 30, 2003. Train robbery in 1921.

"Denison's Ties to the Steamboat *Annie P*," Aug. 3, 2003.

"First Grayson Sheriff [James Mayberry Randolph] Was Appointed, Not Elected," Aug. 31, 2003. Joshua West was first elected sheriff.

"Grave Discovery at Oakwood," July 9, 2003. B.M. Steele, John W. Green, assassination, Chinese tombstone, Dr. Lawrence A. Washington.

"Grayson County History Under Glass," Nov. 12, 2003. Glass positives by Walter P. Lebrecht.

"Grayson's First Sheriff [Joshua West] Quite the Character," July 27, 2003.

"Green Stamps Bring Back Memories," June 1, 2003.

"His Bugle Retired to the Smithsonian Institution," May 25, 2003. Hartley Edwards.

"It Happened a Hundred Years Ago," Dec. 14, 2003. Remembering 1903.

"It [Denison] Was a 'Wild Town' in 1872," Oct. 12, 2003.

"It's Just Like Old Times" (Denton Lunch Bunch, part 1), May 14, 2003.

"Lamar [Elementary School] Students Get a Blast from the Past," Oct. 5, 2003.

"Letter Connects Locals [Scholl and Maughs family] to Civil War Era," Nov. 16, 2003.

"Making the Fire Chief Connections," Sept. 28, 2003. James Cooper, Jones Andrews.

"Marking the [Marcy, Butterfield] Trail to California" (part 1), July 23, 2003. "Trails Marker," Sherman TX.

"Marking the Years" ("Trails Marker," part 2), Aug. 13, 2003.

"[Melvin] Brown Returns to Orange Bowl," Dec. 21, 2003.

"Mistakes Yesterday Are Mistakes Today," Aug. 27, 2003. W.C. Sanders, *Annie P,* Red River navigation.

"Of Colorful Characters and Boneheads [Club of Dallas]," Sept. 3, 2003. Billy Weaver, Dr. H.T. Walker, Mildred Walker, Claud Easterly, Hal Collins.

"Once Upon a Time, a King [Roy Rogers] Walked Among Us," July 6, 2003. Yellow Jacket Boat Company, Billy Holcomb.

"Pat Welch Hamilton Will Be Remembered" (obituary), Oct. 29, 2003.

"[Ralph] Hall Turns 80, Serving Citizens of North Texas," May 6, 2003.

"Rememberin' When," Apr. 27, 2003. Bob Martin, farming at Whitemound.

"Remembering an Old Fire Chief [Joe Capelle]," Sept. 21, 2003.

"Remembering Those 'Momisms'" (part 1), Oct. 19, 2003.

"Rowdy Joe [Lowe] Got Around," Nov. 26, 2003.

"Serving More Nice, Cool Memories [of Ashburn's Creamery]," June 18, 2003.

"[Sheriff Jesse Lee] 'Red' Hall's Hair 'Saved' City from Indians," Dec. 28, 2003.

"The Character(s) of Texoma" (part 1), Aug. 17, 2003.

"The Embers Continue to Glow Brighter Than Ever," Nov. 5, 2003. Bill Russell, Embers Restaurant.

"The Life of Byron [Mitchell] Was a Gas," Dec. 3, 2003. [NOTE: Herald Democrat archive lists as "Lone Star Gas Emergencies."]

"[Theodore] Roosevelt Was Just a Big Ol' Teddy Bear," Apr. 16, 2003. Rough Riders, 1905 visit to Denison and Sherman.

"They Shot the Lights Out in '48," Nov. 9, 2003. Denison football champions.

"Thinking of Sousa's Visits, the Feet Start Tapping," Sept. 7, 2003.

"Those Long-Lasting Friendships" (Denton Lunch Bunch, part 2), May 18, 2003.

"To Thrash or Thresh, That Is the Question," Apr. 30, 2003. [NOTE: Herald Democrat archive lists as "Memories of a Cookshack."]

"We Shall Never Forget: Where Were You the Day President John Kennedy Was Shot?" Nov. 23, 2003.

"When I Was a Little Girl" ("Momisms," part 2), Oct. 22, 2003. Elayne Tignor Vick.

"You Can Come Home Again," Mar. 16, 2003. Donna Hunt returns to newspaper writing.

2004

"114 Years Ago: A Historic Birth [of Dwight David Eisenhower]," Oct. 13, 2004.

"A Bearcat Is a Bearcat Is a Binturong," Nov. 14, 2004. Sherman High School mascot.

"A Hero's Welcome: Changes Abound After 32 Years in Return to Taiwan" (part 1), Jan. 25, 2004. Dr. Judith Thomas.

"[A.R. and Sutton E.] Griggs Looms Large in [Hopewell] Church History," Oct. 20, 2004.

"About the Woman With Five Last Names," Sept. 12, 2004. Sophia Suttonfield Aughinbaugh Coffee Butt Porter.

"Additions Are Music to Our Ears," Mar. 31, 2004. Singer Paula Davis Wendell, Bill Collins, bands, 1949 ice storm, teachers.

"All About George Washington's Kin ... in Denison," Aug. 29, 2004. Dr. Lawrence A. Washington.

"All About 'Spring' Time in Texoma," Oct. 10, 2004. Springs of Grayson County.

"An Epiphany of 'Epiphanies' [Book Store]," Oct. 6, 2004. Karen Jones, Lewis Ray.

"Another Glance at Denison's Early Years" (Tom B. Anderson's memories, part 2), Nov. 28, 2004.

"Another in the Line of Firsts for Denison" (part 1), Aug. 22, 2004. Denison Nelson, Texana Denison McElvany. [NOTE: Herald Democrat archive lists as "First Boy Born in Denison."]

"Back to the Saddle Again," Aug. 15, 2004. Sheriff Woody Blanton.

"Being One of the Chosin Few," Apr. 18, 2004. Korea (1950), Jim Haun, Cecil Carpenter.

"Black and Gold Fever, 20 Years Later," Oct. 31, 2004. DHS 1984 football champions. [NOTE: Herald Democrat archive lists as "Denison Football."]

"Bringing 'Em Back, Over and Over," Apr. 25, 2004. Denison reunions.

"Christmas Steamed in 132 Years Ago," Dec. 26, 2004. First train.

"Citizen [Clara Doherty] Answers Cadet Call," Apr. 28, 2004. Cadet Nurse Corps.

"Classmates Mourn [Olan] Taul" (obituary), June 16, 2004.

"Clora Bryant Was All That Jazz," Jan. 11, 2004.

"Col. [Edwin P. Ramsey] Speaks of Bataan Memories from WWII," June 6, 2004.

"Couple [Judith Thomas, M, Thornberry] Help Professor in His Escape" (Taiwan, part 2), Jan. 27, 2004.

"Courthouse Lawn Surrounded with Mysteries" (part 1), June 20, 2004. [NOTE: Herald Democrat archive lists as "Mystery Cannon on Courthouse Square."]

"Courthouse's Cannon Mysteries Unraveling" (part 2), July 4, 2004.

"Dancing in the [Tropical] Gardens," Feb. 18, 2004. Musician Kenneth Ransom.

"Denison Alumni Honor Four," Sept. 1, 2004. Jerome L. Duggan, Claude H. Organ Jr., Judith Thomas, Don Rice, Melvin Brown.

"Denisonian Confusion," Feb. 11, 2004. George Denison, Dr. Harry Denison and family.

"[Dr. P.T.] Vaught Spread Music Over Local Air Waves" (part 1), Mar. 21, 2004.

"[Dr.] P.T. Vaught Still Stirring Memories" (part 3), Apr. 11, 2004.

"Dust Blow Reveals Birth of Legend: Denison Native ['Tex' O'Reilly] Travels the World," July 14, 2004.

"Ex-Herald Publisher [Cleo B. Crittenden] Dies: Denison Native Began Career in 1948," Dec. 12, 2004.

"From the [James K.] Miller House Springs Denison," Nov. 10, 2004. 1401 W. Walker St.

"Games of Denison Roaring Good Time," Mar. 17, 2004. Lions Club Eyeglasses Project.

"Getting to Know Janet Chambers [DHS Class of 1917]," May 12, 2004.

"Grave Discovery: Father [Neal Henderson], Son Believe They Have Found as Many as 144 Graves" (Brogdon Cemetery, part 1), Sept. 29, 2004.

"Grave Matters and Holy Issues," Sept. 15, 2004. Various cemeteries.

"Harshaw and His Academy," Mar. 7, 2004.

"Has Luck Run Out of the Horseshoe?" Feb. 8, 2004. Life of Benny Binion.

"History Makes Connection: St. Xavier Academy Pieces Past for Son," May 19, 2004.

"History Runs Deep at Brogdon Cemetery" (part 2), Oct. 3, 2004.

"Into the Wild Blue Yonder," Feb. 1, 2004. Perrin Air Force Base Museum.

"It Could've Been Gone, Like the Wind," May 16, 2004. Literary agent Annie Laurie Williams.

"[Judith] Thomas Hero in Taiwan" (part 3), Jan. 28, 2004.

"Just Thinkin' of Old Times," Jan. 4, 2004. Incidents in Denison history.

"Knifemakers [Doyal Nolen, George Nolen] Keep Their Edge" (part 2), July 25, 2004. [NOTE: Herald Democrat archive lists as "Nolen Knives Attract Travel and Collectors."]

"Learn Everything You Need To Know From City Directories," June 13, 2004.

"Life Without 'Spats': Bob Elston, '30s Gangster Re-enactor, Will Be Sorely Missed," July 28, 2004.

"Like Old Times," Jan. 27, 2004. Bill Conatser, football star; chicken hatchery; Tropical Gardens; small trains; train robbery.

"Look for the Burma Shave [Signs]," Jan. 25, 2004.

"Looking Forward to '05 and My Friends [at Herald Democrat]," Dec. 29, 2004. [NOTE: Herald Democrat archives lists as "Favorite Newspaper Employees."]

"Marx Brothers Got Start in Denison," Jan. 7, 2004. [NOTE: Herald Democrat archive lists as "Marx Brothers at the Denison Opera House."]

"McDougall Had His Fingers in a Lot of Denison Pies," Dec. 1, 2004.

"More Cannon Fodder for Grayson Historians," June 27, 2004. Grayson County voted to stay in Union.

"Of City Directories and St. Xavier," June 23, 2004. Grayson County TX GenWeb site, Waltz family, Verein Vorwaerts, St. Xavier's Academy.

"Oh Baby! Denison's First Born" (part 2), Aug. 25, 2004. Denison Nelson, Texana Denison McElvany, Sam Hanna Jr.

"Olive Ann's [Oatman Fairchild] Story: Sherman Woman Survived Family's Massacre and Captivity," Sept. 1, 2004.

"One Man [Obie Greenleaf] Clings to Hope-well," Dec. 12, 2004.

"Passersby Carve Niche for Sand Springs," Oct. 17, 2004.

"Perrin AF Museum Expands at the Base," Oct. 24, 2004.

"Pottsboro Brothers [Doyal Nolen, George Nolen] Are a Cut Above" (part 1), July 21, 2004.[NOTE: Herald Democrat archive lists as "Knife Makers Talented in Many Ways."]

"Remembering Grayson County's Time of Yore" (Tom B. Anderson's memories, part 1), Oct. 27, 2004.

"Return to Sugar Bottom," Aug. 11, 2004. Tom Kellough, Courthouse Square, Michael Quinn Sullivan.

"S&H Green Stamps—Where Have They Gone?" May 30, 2004.

"Singin' the Praises of [Dr.] P.T. Vaught" (part 2), Mar. 25, 2004.

"SOSU Distinguished Alumni Award Given to Denison's [Buddy] Wagner," Sept. 27, 2004.

"St. Patrick's Educating for More Than a Century," July 18, 2004. Sisters of St. Mary of Namur, Belgium.

"Swing Band [Olan Atherton] Felt the Draft in '42," Feb. 29, 2004. Tropical Gardens, singer Paula Davis Wendell.

"Taking a Backward Glance," June 30, 2004. Newspaper highlights from 1873.

"Tapping into Tom's Memory Once Again" (Tom B. Anderson's memories, part 3), Dec. 15, 2004.

"The Ice Storm Cameth in 1949," Feb. 22, 2004.

"'The Infant Wonder' [Denison] Struggled with Social Evils" May 26, 2004.

"The Legend of Jesse James and Big Tree, to Mention Some Names," Dec. 8, 2004.

"The Paper That Binds, an Anniversary Reminds," Aug. 8, 2004. *Denison Herald.*

"The View from the Blacksmith's Shop," May 9, 2004. Charles David Holden.

"The Wonderful World of Miss Nettie Bass," Mar. 3, 2004.

"There's a Story Behind Every Grave," Sept. 5, 2004. Oak Hill Cemetery, Electra Waggoner-Biggs.

"This Antique Rose Is a Real Rambler," Nov. 2, 2004. Vern Mynatt, James K. Miller, Miller Spring, cuttings, genealogy.

"This 'Organ' Beats with a Local Rhythm," May 2, 2004. Dr. Claude Organ Jr.

"Thrill of the Genealogical Hunt," May 5, 2004. James Orin Stinson, portable jail.

"Uncovering Letters at an Old House," Nov. 7, 2004. 1400 W. Walker St., Nancy and Mike McCaughan. [NOTE: Herald Democrat archive lists as "Dr. Paul L. Pierce Home Being Renovated."]

"What Happened to All the Cotton?" Jan. 18, 2004. Industries based on cotton.

"Woman [Mary Ann Bernardin] Carves Niche with Knife Art" (part 3), Aug. 4, 2004. [NOTE: Herald Democrat archive lists as "Talent Runs in Nolen Family."]

2005

"A Bird's-Eye View of History," Mar. 20, 2005. Maps of Denison (1872, 1876, 1886, 1891), Amon Carter Museum, exhibit, website.

"A Flowing Well: [Melvin] Brown Is a Wealth of Information" (Flowing Wells, part 2), June 22, 2005.

"A Note or Two on This [C.J.] Ransom," Apr. 24, 2005.

"A Real Daughter of the Confederacy [Beulah Hull Riddle]," Oct. 26, 2005.

"A Special Thanks," Nov. 27, 2005. [NOTE: Herald Democrat archive lists as "Heritage Park Flagpole Honors James 'Pancho' Goddard."]

"A Stitch in Time: St. Luke's Rector [Rev. Curt Norman] Digs Up a Warm Reminder of Denison's Past," Aug. 31, 2005. Billy Bird Jackson, quilt.

"A Story of Thievery, a Century Ago," Nov. 30, 2005. Sherman TX burglary (1904), lawman shot.

"A Tough Time Remembered," June 15, 2005. Bobby Lee Spencer murdered (1978).

"Ah, Those Little Neighborhood Stores," Nov. 20, 2005. Schools, lunches, store owners.

"Ahh, the Good Ol' Days of 'Mom and Pop' Stores," June 9, 2005. Loi-Mac Drug Store.

"All the Presidents' People" (part 1), Dec. 4, 2005. U.S. Presidents who visited Grayson County.

"Ambrose [TX] Was Once a Trade Center," Mar. 16, 2005.

"And Speaking of Gas ... " (Tom B. Anderson's memories, part 5), Aug. 17, 2005. Vin Fiz, Mildred Walker, industries.

"And the Bands Played On," Feb. 27, 2005. Musical groups.

"Bible's Genesis: The Family Behind the Start of Ambrose, Texas," Mar. 30, 2005.

"Big Tree, Big Trouble" (part 2), Jan. 9, 2005. Satanta, Big Tree.

"Bridging the Past," Sept. 7, 2005. Carpenter's Bluff.

"Buildings Honoring Flyers Standing Strong," Jan. 16, 2005. Perrin Air Force Base, Grayson College.

"Catching Up with the 'Gang'" (part 2), May 25, 2005. Little Rascals filmed in Denison.

"Cherry-Pickin': Wading Through Memories with Mr. Denison's [Bob Cherry] Family," Aug. 3, 2005.

"Choctaw Chose to Follow Code [A Life for a Life]," Mar. 2, 2005. Story by Jerry Lincecum.

"Church on Wheels Makes Way Across Tracks," July 10, 2005.

"Condemned Choctaw [Murderer] Meets Fate," Feb. 16, 2005. Death ritual.

"Country Legend [Chris LeDoux] Was a Hometown Boy," May 11, 2005. Donis Kay McBee Henson, "Our Gang."

"Craving Those Durham Burgers" (part 1), Oct. 30, 2005.

"Delivering Denison: Post Office Construction Began 95 Years Ago," Oct. 6, 2005.

"Dictation Program Just Not My Type," July 14, 2005. Surgery, German POWs.

"Distinguished DHS Alumni," Sept. 21, 2005. Billy Bird Jackson, David Bryant, Jack Hicks, Jack Lilley, Gil A. "Sonny" Stricklin, Gaylon

Don Taylor Jr., Dr. Frances Cornell Willis, Roy Sims "Butch" Goodman Jr., 1953 Yellow Jacket Band.

"Faces from the Past Emerge," Apr. 3, 2005. DHS Class of 1911.

"He [Ken Miller] Colored the Planes That Won the War," Dec. 7, 2005.

"Ike's Pomp and Circumstance Recalled," Jan. 30, 2005. DHS Yellow Jacket Band, 1953 Presidential Inauguration.

"Interesting Characters Dot Denison's Past," Oct. 9, 2005. Doc Holliday.

"Jurassic Reminder," Dec. 18, 2005. Ron and Donna Bartee, giant marine predator, bones.

"Just Check the Local [1891-92] City Directory," Mar. 27, 2005.

"Kiowa Chiefs Made Whistle Stops in Denison" (part 1), Jan. 5, 2005. Satanta, Big Tree.

"Legendary Lawman [Bass Reeves] Has Local Ties," Aug. 10, 2005.

"Man [Chris Bowling] Still Haunted by Experience with Prison Escapees [11 May 1978]," May 22, 2005.

"Marching for Ike," Sept. 21, 2005. DHS Yellow Jacket Band, presidential inauguration.

"Marching On at Calvary [Baptist Church]," Nov. 16, 2005. Founded 1905.

"Memories Remain: Former Resident Recalls Days 'High on a Windy Hill'," Apr. 20, 2005. Woodmen Circle Home.

"More About Those Who Served" ("Under the Colors," part 2), Sept. 11, 2005.

"New Year, New Home: Take a Look Back at a Family [E.J. Smith] Moving to Denison in Dec. 1876," Dec. 29, 2005. Train wreck, arrival, description.

"Of Villains and Heroines," Feb. 6, 2005. Photos, Satanta, Big Tree, Satank, Mae Mosse, Anna Mosse, Edna Clara Mosse, B.C. Murray, L.S. Owings, teachers.

"Off the Tracks for 40 Years," July 20, 2005. End of Katy passenger service (1 July 1965).

"Ol' Tom's Memories of Denison" (Tom B. Anderson's memories, part 6), Aug. 28, 2005.

"Pondering Denison's Connection with 'Our Gang'" (part 1), May 15, 2005. Harold Eugene Wertz Jr., Little Rascals, filming in Forest Park.

"Presidential Memories" (part 2), Dec. 11, 2005. Harry Truman (1947, 1961).

"Recalling [Gene] Autry and 'The Big Show'," June 12, 2005. Texas Centennial, Billy Holcomb, film extra Raymond Smith.

"Remembering a Face from the Past [musician Gustave William Sommerfeldt]," Mar. 6, 2005.

"Remembering a Face in the Band [Linnstaedts]," July 24, 2005.

"Remembering a Local WWII Veteran [Allen Allender]," June 1, 2005.

"Remembering the Days of Paperboys," Apr. 27, 2005.

"Remembering 'Under the Colors'" (part 1), Sept. 4, 2005. World War II.

"Scattershooting Across Several Columns," Aug. 7, 2005. Goebel Reeves, Col. George R. Reeves, artist Louise French, musician Emil Carl Linsteadt.

"She Caught the Katy," Jan. 23, 2005. Dining car, onion soup, Patrick H. Tobin (obituary).

"Sherman Tie to Famous Musician [Goebel Reeves]," July 31, 2005.

"Side of Memories, Hold the Mayo" (Durham Burgers, part 2), Nov. 9, 2005. Durham's Hamburgers, Wiest Grocery, Minnie Coffman.

"Sophia [Suttonfield Aughinbaugh Coffee Butt] Porter Among County's Most Colorful Pioneers," Mar. 13, 2005.

"The 'Big Story' 27 Years Ago," May 18, 2005. McAlester OK prison escapees, 26 May 1978, Bobby Lee Spencer killed.

"The Diamond Was This Girl's [Mary Waitman] Best Friend," Aug. 24, 2005. Baseball.

"The Light of Denison's Early Black Schools," Feb. 13, 2005.

"The Mystery with the UFO Story" (part 3), Oct. 23, 2005.

"The Red Ink of Red River City," Feb. 20, 2005. Colbert's Red River Record, building of Denison Dam.

"The Shot Heard 'Round Fannin County," Aug. 21, 2005. Lee-Peacock feud.

"The Wells Were Flowing Back Then" (Flowing Wells, part 1), May 29, 2005. Pearsons, 4th of July.

"They Gave So Much," Nov. 11, 2005. Veterans Day, bugler Hartley Edwards, James "Pancho" Goddard.

"Tidbits From School Days Past," Nov. 2, 2005. Central Ward School, Educational Institute, Historic DHS, Sherman school for freed slaves, first time a Texas school board buys football equipment.

"Tracking Down the H&TC Railroad Heroine," Jan. 26, 2005. Train wreck (1898), Mae Mosse, Anna Mosse, John Day Daffin, Central Ward Elementary School.

"Trying to Explain the 'Unexplained'" (part 1), Oct. 2, 2005. UFO sightings near Bonham (1873), Denison (1878 and 1981), Perrin AFB (1953).

"UFOs Just What Name Implies, Says Perrin Veteran" (part 2), Oct. 16, 2005.

"Well-Traveled, 99-Year-Old Lola Mae Hensley [Stevens] Is Still Ready To Go," Mar. 9, 2005.

"When the [German] POWs Were at Lake Texoma," June 19, 2005.

"Writings from a Jogged Memory," May 1, 2005. Austin Harshbarger, Hagerman TX, Gustave William Sommerfeldt, Milton Joseph Burton, Susie Marie Potter Burton, bridge passes, Lola Mae Stevens.

"'You Can Be Content'," Mar. 23, 2005. Aliwilda Mae Blain, Baptist Orphan's Home, Ambrose TX.

"You Could Get All You Wanted for 50 Cents" (Tom B. Anderson's memories, part 4), Aug. 14, 2005. Vin Fiz, businesses, railroads, town leaders, visiting dignitaries, Oak View Inn, musicians.

2006

"A Modern Swing to the Old LPs: '80s Music Scene One of the Best in Denison," Mar. 8, 2006.

"A Snapshot of Main, from the 200 Block of History," Mar. 15, 2006.

"All the King's Horses and All the King's Men," Mar. 29, 2006. [NOTE: Herald Democrat archive lists as "Justin Raynal and His Monument."]

"And the Streets Were Paved in Brick," Oct. 8, 2006. Thurber bricks, Serpentine Main St.

"Back in Denison's Mill Days," Nov. 19, 2006. Industry. [NOTE: Herald Democrat archive lists as "Denison Was a Cotton Mill Town."]

"Before the Interurban, There Was the 'Dinkey'," Oct. 29, 2006.

"Behind the Legend of Sugar Bottom," July 16, 2006.

"Birthplace the Center of Ike's History Today" (part 6), Mar. 26, 2006.

"Catching Up with Friends and Events," Jan. 11, 2006. Dorothy P. Marks, Perrin Air Force Base, Nelita P. Bruno, Goebel Reeves, Jerry Durham, Tom Price, Sugar Bottom, Lavada Cuthbertson, baking.

"Catching Up With Short Messages," June 2, 2006. Denison bottling companies, fiddles, haunted house, Hendrix House, Bertha Knaur Johnson, E.G. Johnson, G.P. Brous, James Gerard Gorman, icehouse, teachers, Red River Story Tellers.

"Chinese Tombstone Brings Out History of the Orient in Texoma," July 12, 2006. Oakwood Cemetery, Dr. Lloyd W.C. Tang. [NOTE: Discussed here is another article, "Mystery in Oakwood [Cemetery]: Early-Day Denison Tombstone Deciphered," Apr. 7, 1968.]

"Coming Home: Dwight Eisenhower Is Elected President, but Does Not Carry the Vote in Denison, Where He Was Born" (part 4), Mar. 12, 2006.

"Coverage of KKK [Ku Klux Klan] in the '20s Extended Beyond the Public Eye" (part 2), May 28, 2006. Dr. Donna Kumler, Alexander Bates, William Hill, Sherman's black business district.

"Denison Has a History with Drug Stores [Kingston's, Loi-Mac, Harris]," Dec. 10, 2006.

"Denison Has Connection to State of Colorado," Sept. 21, 2006. Rod and Gun Club.

"Denison Man's [Theodore "Ted" Schirmer] Memory Kept Alive with Paintings," June 25, 2006.

"Denisonians Involved in Nation's History," Mar. 1, 2006. Adm. Adolphus Andrews, Berenice Platter Andrews.

"Eisenhower's Legacy Continues Today" (part 5), Mar. 19, 2006.

"Enjoy the 4th of July: Celebrations in Denison's Past [1876]," July 2, 2006.

"Finding Answers: This and That About Area History," July 6, 2006. White Pig, snow on July 4 [at Flowing Wells], Ku Klux Klan, "interesting character" Bill Darby, Col. Paul Waples.

"First Old Settlers [Association] Picnicked in 1879," Feb. 9, 2006.

"Flag [actually *Stars and Stripes* newspaper] Shows Pivotal Points in World War II," June 11, 2006.

"Flood of Memories Jogged by Recent Tales," Aug. 13, 2006. Historic DHS, McDaniel Junior High School, Interurban, railroad roundhouse and turntable.

"Flowing Wells Brings Back Memories for Texoma Residents" (part 2), July 19, 2006.

"Frontier Village Stirs Memories," Apr. 9, 2006. DHS Yearbooks (1914, 1915), wolf hunt, baseball, concert band, Woodlake, Laura Doak Bell, Lula Mae Hays, Edith Austin.

"Full Service: Reminiscing About a Vanishing Piece of Americana—The Filling Station: $2 To Buy a Week's Worth of Gasoline," Aug. 23, 2006. List of service stations (1940), McKee Brothers.

"Harry Gaines' Letter Recalls Denison's Sugar Bottom," Jan. 22, 2006.

"Historical Information Rises to the Surface," Nov. 15, 2006. "Old Stoneface," Dinkey (train), Aaron Witz AKA David A. Witts.

"History Unearthed," Jan. 22, 2006. Ron and Donna Bartee, Sam Noble Oklahoma Museum of Natural History, Charles McLin, giant marine reptile, bones.

"Humble Beginnings: From His Birth in a Rental House in Denison, Dwight David Eisenhower Grew To Put His Stamp on Our World" (part 1), Feb. 19, 2006.

"If Only the Interurban Still Ran" (part 2), Aug. 6, 2006.

"Ike on Postage Stamps" (part 7), Mar. 26, 2006.

"In Highway Infancy, the Jefferson [Highway] Wound Through Texoma," Dec. 17, 2006. Map.

"Interurban Brings Back Memories" (part 1), Aug. 2, 2006.

"Katy Book [*Miss Katy in the Lone Star State*] Revisits Railroad," Aug. 16, 2006. Steve Goen.

"Lady Bird [Johnson] a Texas Legend," Jan. 6, 2006.

"Letter from Mom Sets Ike Straight" (part 3), Mar. 5, 2006.

"Life Before the Chain Restaurant: Celebrating the Hangouts of the Past," May 10, 2006. White Pig, Johnny McCraw, Carl McCraw.

"Looking Back to Christmas Past," Dec. 21, 2006. First train, Patrick H. Tobin, R.L. Anderson, first Christmas dinner, Jack Maguire, 60th anniversary (1932), 70th anniversary (1942), World War II.

"Mailbag Brings Flood of Memories from Readers," Aug. 30, 2006. Security Building, Bluebonnet Cafe, Dr. Claud Crawford, Interurban, McKee Brothers Service Station, Bob Cosby.

"Many Memories Were Formed at Woodlake," Oct. 25, 2006.

"McKinney Man [Dick Wickel AKA Wyk Wight] on a Dam Mission," Sept. 3, 2006. George D. Moulton, Fran Higginbotham, Otis Higginbotham, Baer's Ferry.

"Mementos of the Area's Earliest Settlers" (part 1), Oct. 1, 2006. Dugan family of Bells TX, Indian's skull, Fitzgerald House at Frontier Village. [NOTE: Errors in this column corrected Oct. 4, 2006.]

"Memories Paved with Thurber Bricks," Oct. 18, 2006. Thurber TX, Lillis Lane, Jess R. Redmon's small train at 731 W. Crawford St., Belgians search for local veterans.

"[Milton] Taul Celebrates 95 Years," Apr. 6, 2006.

"More Remembrances about Flowing Wells" (part 1), July 9, 2006. [NOTE: Article cited: 29 May 2005.]

"News of [Historic Denison High] School's Demise Opens Trove of Memories," July 30, 2006.

"Newspaper Ink in the Easterly Family Blood," Aug. 20, 2006.

"Nothing Ventured, Nothing 'Gained'," Jan. 15, 2006. Dee Gaines, Harry Gaines, Denison memorabilia.

"Paperhangers Cause Weekend Speculation," Jan. 18, 2006. Pranks, Daffan-Geisenhoner marriage license, flags on viaduct.

"Papers Reveal Doctor's [Dr. Alexander W. Acheson] Life During Civil War," May 17, 2006.

"'Porching It' Proves Sage Advice," Aug. 9, 2006. Joel Ward, Burris Hughes, *Denison Herald*, newspaper carriers, rules, life lessons.

"R.C. Vaughan's Historical Legacy," Nov. 19, 2006.

"Recollections of Those Who've Passed," Feb. 12, 2006. Coretta Scott King, Dorothy Cobb, Martin Kohl, Lyndon Hyatt, Bea Spangler.

"[Red River] Railroad Museum Still Relevant, Needs Help," Nov. 12, 2006.

"Remembering and Admiring [Texas Gov.] Ann Richards," Sept. 17, 2006. [NOTE: This column has an error, corrected on Sept. 24, 3006. Ann Richards not first female elected governor of Texas.]

"Remembering Bloomfield Academy from Long Ago," Oct. 22, 2006.

"Remembering Denison's Colorful History" ("Night of Terror," part 1), Nov. 22, 2006.

"Remembering One of the Area's First 'Spas'," Sept. 6, 2006. Jacobs Hotel, Milo Jacobs.

"Remembering the Importance of Voting," Nov. 5, 2006. Elizabeth Bledsoe, Jennie Jackson, teachers.

"Renewing the Pioneer Spirit; [Davis-Ansley] Cabin Is Historical," Apr. 26, 2006. Evelyn and Wendell Brown. [NOTE: Herald Democrat archive lists as "Davis Descendant Wed at Frontier Village."]

"She Gave a New 'Lease' on Life for Women," Oct. 11, 2006. Mary Elizabeth Lease, WCTU, Populist Party, Sarah C. Acheson, Dorothy Rose Blumberg (author).

"Slick DHS Magazine [*Traditions*] Now Out," Jan. 8, 2006. Denison Alumni Association.

"Slingin' the Hash," Dec. 6, 2006. Johnny McCraw, cafe "slanguage," restaurants.

"Standing Guard for More Than a Century," Nov. 8, 2006. Fairview Cemetery, Grand Army of the Republic (GAR), Union Soldier statue, rededication.

"Still Musing About the Corner Markets," Apr. 23, 2006. Small grocery stores, two women named "Nondas," Dwight D. Eisenhower and Denison men on *USS Helena* in 1952.

"Taking a Bus Trip Back in Time," Sept. 10, 2006. DHS, Latin class, Spanish class, Edith Austin, Mildred Walker, convention, missed bus, wild time.

"Texas Giants: Story of the Shields Is a Tall Tale, Yes, But Also a Very True Tale," June 7, 2006. Jack Shields, one of four giant brothers, visited Denison in 1880.

"That First Train [1872]," Dec. 27, 2006. Mrs. Bill Linden (1947 interview), camping in Forest Park, housing, cholera epidemic, "Night of Terror."

"The Bell Tolls for Old Denison High School [on Main Street]," July 26, 2006.

"The Depth of the KKK [Ku Klux Klan] Back in the Day" (part 1), May 24, 2006. Dr. Donna Kumler, origins, Sherman activities.

"The Final Events in Denison's Night of Terror" (part 3), Nov. 29, 2006.

"The Old War Ties That Bind," Sept. 24, 2006. Belgian man seeks relatives of Marion E. Flanery, WWII veteran buried in Collinsville Cemetery; Bertie Oldham's diamonds; Texas Gov. Ma Ferguson.

"The Story of the Area's Rough Frontier Past Continues" (part 2), Oct. 4, 2006. Emily Dugan, Daniel Vaden Dugan, William Kitching, Indians, Rangers, Samuel Johnson.

"The Story on Goebel Reeves' Lineage," Jan. 1, 2006. Musician.

"The Unfolding Events in Denison's Night of Terror" (part 2), Nov. 26, 2006.

"They Made Their Mark," Jan. 8, 2006. DHS teachers, Elizabeth Bledsoe, Maggie Sommerville, "Spanish Armada, 1588," awards, world travelers.

"This Building's Tale Has Many 'Stories'," Aug. 27, 2006. Security Building, "Old Stoneface," professional offices, Bluebonnet Cafe, demolition (1954), Lilley-Linn Department Store.

"Triple Digits: 102-Year-Old Alice Cox Offered Sage Advice to Those Attending Benefit for Denison Scholarship Fund," June 28, 2006. Grew up in Denison.

"What's in a Street Name? More Than You Think," Feb. 5, 2006.

"When Eisenhower Set the Record Straight" (part 2), Feb. 26, 2006.

"WWII War Artist [Ken Miller] Shows Work Saturday," Nov. 10, 2006.

"Yes, Virginia, There Is a Santa Claus," Dec. 24, 2006.

2007

"A Christmas Story Tells of Simpler Times from Long Ago," Dec. 24, 2007. From DHS *Raven* (Dec. 1903). [NOTE: Herald Democrat archive lists as "A Christmas Story Years in the Making."]

"A Sampling of Grayson History" (Chronology, 1859 to 1873), Nov. 25, 2007.

"Camp Fire USA Denison Loses Local Funding, Closes Doors," Apr. 4, 2007.

"Chance Meetings Form Meaningful Bonds," Feb. 7, 2007. Royden L. Lebrecht donates to Collin County Community College.

"Communities Banding Together for a Common Purpose," Sept. 16, 2007. Historic DHS, Galena IL, Melinda Mayes Penn.

"D-Day Story Draws Flurry of Comments" (part 2), June 13, 2007.

"Denison Has Experienced Many Memorable 'Firsts'," May 24, 2007. Fire truck, First State Bank (Ford Building), Mrs. A.H. Coffin, Harrison Tone, Dwight D. Eisenhower, ice cream soda, Theodore Roosevelt's visit (1905), Joseph A. Euper, Forest Park, Vin Fiz.

"Denison Loses Prominent Resident [Laverne Marguerite Bradshaw]" (obituary), Jan. 28, 2007. Musician, teacher, Terrell High School.

"Denison Native [Penny Farrington] Excels in California Police Work," Jan. 24, 2007. Bonnie Parker, Clyde Barrow, African American librarian Gertrude Bruce, Thelma Harris.

"Denison Proud of the Many Historical Sites," Sept. 2, 2007. Joseph A. Euper, Joseph G. McCoy, Chisholm Trail, Eisenhower Birthplace, Historic Denison High School, tourism.

"Denison Schools, the Early Years," Mar. 28, 2007.

"Denison's [Joseph G.] McCoy and His Ties to the Chisholm Trail," Sept. 19, 2007.

"Denisonians Make Great Achievements," May 9, 2007. John W. Barringer III National Railroad Library (St. Louis MO), artist Al Clymer.

"[DHS] Class of '42 Affected by Pearl Harbor," Dec. 7, 2007. Dr. Dorothy Hawkins Rushing.

"Discovering Denison's History of Loy Lake Park," Oct. 14, 2007.

"Discovering Pieces of Denison's Past," Sept. 23, 2007. Martin Patti Sr., *Red River* premier, TV exec Phil Hurley, artist Willard Cooper.

"Discovering the Past in Whitewright," June 3, 2007.

"Finding the Old Hyde Park School" (part 1), Nov. 7, 2007. Sarah Dye, Y-Teen Cup found, Caroline Neu's mystery painting.

"From Trails to Superhighways," July 29, 2007. Gainesville TX Centennial (1948), map.

"Going Way Back into Texoma's History" (Chronology, 1542 to 1846), Nov. 18, 2007.

"Gravesites Need Attention, Maintenance," Aug. 1, 2007. Preston Bend Cemetery Association, Sophia Suttonfield Aughinbaugh Coffee Butt Porter, Holland Coffee, pet cemetery.

"High School Yearbooks Take Us on a Trip Through the Past," Mar. 18, 2007.

"History of PTA in Denison Reviewed," June 20, 2007.

"Jesse and Frank James Had Strong Connections to Grayson County," Jan. 31, 2007.

"Lack of Water in Denison Never a Problem," Dec. 2, 2007. Waterloo Lake, Randell Lake, Drought of 1909, fires, fire bell.

"Life Under the Big Top in Texoma," Jan. 21, 2007. Gainesville Circus, Frank Buck Zoo.

"Little Words Lead to Big Stories," May 18, 2007. Sherman Cyclone (1896), L.F. Ely's wardrobe, John Tate, Lee-Peacock feud, biographies of area people (1920s).

"Local NAACP 'Closing the Gap' [between Denison and Sherman]," Mar. 2, 2007. Baseball, Roger Williams, Curtis Moore, Alvin Dunlap, JoAnn Perkins, Black History.

"Looking Back at D-Day" (part 1), June 6, 2007. Johnny Goldston, Claude Woodley.

"Looking Back on Denison Disasters," Mar. 4, 2007. Butane explosion (1944), Denison Dam spillway (1957 and 1990), "pop corn guy" Harry C. Brown, Hitch Grounds in Sherman.

"Looking Over the Fence, Historically Speaking," Feb. 11, 2007. Tom Bomar recalls early Sherman TX.

"Looking to 'Uncover' the History of Old Railroad Graveyard," Aug. 29, 2007. MKT Railroad's graveyard for amputated human limbs, Henry B. Sanborn's ranch, barbed wire, Historic Denison High School, demolition, clock, teachers, Stella Byers, Layne School.

"Memories of Grocery Stores Are All That Remain from Years Ago," Feb. 21, 2007. "The Jockey Lot," 100 block W. Woodard St., "pop corn guy," Hitch Grounds in Sherman, Oleta Singleton's taxi.

"Memories of JKF Assassination in Dallas," Nov. 29, 2007.

"National Pastime Part of Early Denison History," Feb. 18, 2007. [NOTE: Herald Democrat archive lists as "Baseball Teams."]

"Notorious Ties to Grayson County," Jan. 17, 2007. Raymond Hamilton, Clyde Barrow.

"Old [Denison High] School's Clock Evokes Memories of Donor [R.D. Beirne] from Early 20th Century," Nov. 11, 2007.

"Old Tree on Old [Denison] High School Building Site Being Dismantled," July 8, 2007. Old trees, Bill Brown, C.W. "Corn" Colbert, Indian Territory, hanging tree, stolen horse.

"Ophelia's Life Story Shines Next to Two Good Men [W.R. "Bill" Taylor, Claud Easterly]," Aug. 5, 2007. Teacher, Peabody Elementary School, banker Bill Martin, Ranch Style Beans, Vest Brothers Grocery, Carl's Cafe.

"Peace Officers Give Their Lives in the Line of Duty for Grayson County," Apr. 8, 2007. Marshal Jim Isbell killed (1891), John Martin a hero, Mr. "Smith" hanged.

"Preston [Bend] Important to History of the Area," Nov. 4, 2007.

"Putting Names to the Faces," Oct. 17, 2007. Denison High School, reunions, class photos.

"Ranch Style Beans' Roots in Denison," July 22, 2007. [NOTE: Herald Democrat archive lists as "Denison Has Celebrated Many Firsts."]

"Readers Share More Memories of Elvis" (part 2), Aug. 23, 2007. Jerry Hatfield's photo in *Life* magazine (16 June 1972).

"Recalling DHS' Most Famed Band Director [Neil Shirley]," Aug. 19, 2007.

"Recalling the Days of [Nall] Drug Store Yore," Aug. 12, 2007. Sherman TX, Judge Rim Nall.

"Remembering Grayson County History" (Chronology, 1859 to 1900), Dec. 30, 2007.

"Remembering [Hyde Park] School Days" (part 2), Nov. 15, 2007. "Miss Bettie" (cook), "Brother Bob" AKA "PaPaw," Cashion School.

"Remembering the Central Ward [School] in Denison," May 20, 2007.

"Remembering the Crash at Crush," Feb. 4, 2007.

"Reporter [Claud Easterly] Looks Back on School Days of Old in Denison," June 28, 2007.

"Sanborn Ranch [near Whitesboro] Has Connection to State Fair," Oct. 24, 2007.

"School Days [at Historic DHS] Remembered with Fondness," Sept. 30, 2007. Clock tower, bell, donor R.D. Beirne, demolition.

"Sherman's 1896 Cyclone Remembered" (part 1), Apr. 15, 2007.

"Son of Former Oklahoma Governor [Raymond Gary] Lives in Denison," Oct. 31, 2007. Jerdy Gary.

"Sophia [Suttonfield Aughinbaugh Coffee Butt Porter], Heroine of Glen Eden, Had Five Last Names," Mar. 21, 2007.

"Teaching an Old Dogma New Tricks," Mar. 7, 2007. Virginia Point UMC, digital hymnal.

"Tearing Down Old Memories," June 10, 2007. Historic Denison High School, demolition.

"Texoma Holiday Magazine a Hit in 1948," July 15, 2007.

"The Mission: Looking for the Y-Teen Cup," Oct. 28, 2007. Denison High School.

"The Peacock in the Corners," May 6, 2007. Lee-Peacock feud.

"The Train Robberies of the MKT [1901 and 1921]," Jan. 10, 2007. Denison Bank & Trust.

"They Had Nothing to Fear But Fear Itself," Dec. 12, 2007. *Denison Herald* on Pearl Harbor events.

"Things Are Changing Around Texoma, Critters Disappearing," Apr. 11, 2007.

"To Always Remember, Never Forget," May 27, 2007. Memorial Day, Hartley Edwards, Fairview Cemetery, World War I casualties.

"To Market, to Market ... in Sherman-Denison," Feb. 14, 2007. Hitch Grounds in Sherman, Casteel Grocery, W.H. Lucas grocery stores, W.R. Allen Cash Grocery, Denison's trade grounds, 100 and 200 blocks W. Woodard St.

"Tragic Events Remain a Clear Memory," Nov. 25, 2007. John F. Kennedy assassination.

"Treasures Left Behind by 1896 Tornado" (part 2), May 2, 2007. Sherman Cyclone, L.F. Ely, Jenny Pack Omundson, wardrobe, brick, "Preacher" (shoe-shine man), Sam Pack.

"Trying to Save a Little Bit of Denison History," June 24, 2007. Historic Denison High School, demolition, clock tower, artist Janet Karam.

"U.S. Army Honors Denison Women," Mar. 18, 2007. U.S. Army Field Band, African American female musicians Marva Lewis, Helen Cole, Marguerite Bradshaw.

"Virginia Man [Catlett James Atkins] Settles in Grayson County," Mar. 11, 2007. Chief justice of Grayson County (1857-58).

"Where the Buffalo Roam," Jan. 14, 2007. Judge J.P. Simpson, buffalo hunt, sale of buffalo hides in Grayson County in 1870s, map. [NOTE: Another article, published on May 24, 2006, has the same title. It is not the same article, however.]

"Wolfe City Man [John "Dub" Duncan] Shares Hometown History," June 17, 2007. *Wolfe City Mirror*, musical groups.

"Working Hard May Be Secret To Living a Longer Life," Sept. 9, 2007. Martin Patti Sr., Jennie Bruno, grapes, T.V. Munson, World War II.

2008

"'A Busy, Progressive City with Golden Opportunities'" (part 1), Aug. 17, 2008. Booklet titled "Denison, the Texas Gateway" (1907); MKT Railroad reunion; residents and their businesses.

"A 'Little Pat' for the American Legion," Mar. 2, 2008. Ray West made miniature train (1951).

"Another 'Grape' Man [Elbert W. Kirkpatrick] from Sherman-Denison Area" (part 2), Feb. 20, 2008. Confederate veteran was a McKinney horticulturist who owned Texas Nursery Company in Sherman and was T.V. Munson's friend.

"Athletes Horsed Around in Denison of Yesteryear," June 18, 2008. Polo, starting in 1874. [NOTE: Herald Democrat archive lists as "Early Polo Team."]

"Building Downtown Denison Brick by Brick, 1907" (part 5), Sept. 12, 2008. Booklet titled "Denison, the Texas Gateway" (1907); brick streets laid 1907; local businesses.

"Church Origins Prove Fascinating," Nov. 9, 2008. Presbyterians, St. Luke's, Catholics, Hopewell Baptist, First Christian, Methodists, Baptists.

"Civil War—A Generation Removed," Aug. 24, 2008. Beulah Hull Riddle and Lydia Jane Snavely.

"Civilian Conservation Corps Leaves Its Mark in Grayson County," Feb. 10, 2008. Loy Lake Park.

"Clothes for the Worker, Made in Texoma," Apr. 16, 2008. Pool Manufacturing, Patterson Manufacturing, Levi Strauss.

"Cotton Mill Memories Abound in Denison," Oct. 26, 2008. James Burden worked at mill, lived nearby.

"Crawford Street Subway," Mar. 30, 2008. Double underpasses, Rep. Vernon Beckham.

"Curious Minds Want to Know—About Historical Markers" (part 1), July 6, 2008. Texas-shaped stone marker, Jerry Simpson, Denison Dam, U.S. Army Corps of Engineers.

"Deep into Denison's Sports History," July 2, 2008. Gate City Baseball Association, Denison Baseball Association, Railroaders, noted players, Mortimer M. "Snake Editor" Scholl.

"Delaware Bend Has Rich, Colorful History," May 21, 2008.

"Denison Barber Shop Has Early History" (part 3), Sept. 3, 2008. Booklet titled "Denison, the Texas Gateway" (1907); residents and their businesses; early-day baseball.

"Denison Home to Number of Manufacturers," Jan. 24, 2008. *The Denison Guide* (1939), Kraft Cheese, Denison Cotton Mill, flour mills, brick, Gate City Hosiery Mill, Jaques Power Saw, W.J. Smith Wood Preserving, Peanut Processing, Levi Strauss, others.

"Denison Man [Thomas Gibbs Johnson] Served with Sergeant York in World War I," Nov. 23, 2008. Sgt. Alvin York did not fight alone.

"Denison Names Distinguished Alumni, Inducts into Sports Hall of Fame," Aug. 22, 2008. Edmond Ellis, Dr. Linda Chapman Medearis, Waldene Trim Nevil, Horace Groff, Natalie Polk Cobb, Aaron Jackson, Coach M.M. Marshall.

"Denison Natives Living in California Hold Annual Denison Reunion," May 8, 2008.

"Denison Strives To Be Progressive in 1912," Mar. 9, 2008. Crawford Street Subway (underpass), first fire truck, school outhouses. [NOTE: Herald Democrat archive lists as "Progressive Is In the Eye of the Beholder."]

"Denison, in the Time of Cholera [1873]," Apr. 13, 2008. Dr. Alexander W. Acheson, Dr. James Johnston, Mrs. Bill Linden, malaria.

"Denison's History Filled With Music," Dec. 14, 2008. Opera houses, Marx Brothers.

"DHS Lunch Bunch," Apr. 20, 2008. Honoring DHS Classes of 1948 and 1958.

"Discovering the Mystery of [Paul] Borum's Tower," Mar. 22, 2008. First Denison police radio tower, Municipal Building, Alice Bryant, Harry Tone, Tone Abstract Company, "The Medicine Man."

"Drug Stores Were the Anchors of Bygone Main Streets" (part 4), Sept. 7, 2008. Booklet titled "Denison, the Texas Gateway" (1907); bicycle shop; caterer; pharmacies.

"Early Crafts That Sailed Across Lake Texoma," July 27, 2008. John Clift, Wanderer, Moulton, Idle Time, Island Queen.

"[Elbert W.] Kirkpatrick's History" (part 1), Feb. 17, 2008. Steve Hutchison investigates a Confederate veteran of McKinney TX.

"Flour Sacks Served Double Purpose During Depression," Mar. 19, 2008. Many uses. [NOTE: Herald Democrat archive lists as "The Age of the Flour Sack."]

"Following the Shawnee Trail through Grayson County," May 18, 2008. Preston Poad, Shawneetown, map.

"Food Brings Back Fond Memories," May 28, 2008. Bakeries, Ballard's Biscuits, Pillsbury, Cagle's, Crane's. [NOTE: Herald Democrat archive lists as "Ah, the Smell of Freshly Baked Bread," May 25, 2008.]

"Four Carnegie Hero Medals Earned by Denison Residents," Nov. 19, 2008. Clarence Farris, Henry L. Halliday, Wayne Ramsey, Marvin Ray Griffith.

"Gas Prices Are a Pain in the Pump," June 1, 2008.

"Getting Help from the Unlikeliest Places," Mar. 5, 2008. PO Sam's Barbecue, Colbert OK, computers, newspaper typesetting.

"Honoring Local Veterans," Nov. 30, 2008. "Under the Colors" (special edition of *Denison Herald*, Labor Day, 1943), military, home front, unions, lodges, churches, casualties.

"Infamous Belle Starr Spent Time in Denison" (part 2), Oct. 5, 2008. Mortimer M. "Snake Editor" Scholl.

"[John Earl] Jaques Invented Circular Saw, Used to Clear Land for Lake Texoma," Apr. 23, 2008.

"Local Finds Famous Genealogical Ties," Oct. 12, 2008. Dr. Lawrence A. Washington.

"Looking Back at Denison's History," Jan. 27, 2008. Mortimer M. "Snake Editor" Scholl, Red River navigation, *Annie P* (boat), *Denison Dispatch, Historic Denison*.

"Made in Texoma, Made in America," Feb. 6, 2008. Buy local, go green.

"'Magnificent Flour Mill' Part of Denison History," Mar. 26, 2008. Lone Star Mills, W.B. Boss, J.W. Jennings, cornerstone, James T. Williams, C.B. Sullenberger, grist mill.

"Man [Glen Ely] Tells the Tale of the Butterfield Overland Mail Route," Sept. 28, 2008.

"Memorial Day: Local Veteran [Bill Russell] Remembered," May 26, 2008. Embers Restaurant.

"Memories of Christmas Past," Dec. 17, 2008. Nativity scene at Katy Car Shops, Santa stand-ins, Christmas Eve gatherings, allergies, tree, church events, parade.

"More on the Bush Swimming Pool Family" (part 2), Oct. 29, 2008. Bush family home (1700 block W. Johnson St.), fire (Jan. 1939), rescue by Walter Armstrong. [NOTE: This article corrects errors in article published Oct. 19, 2008.]

"More to Know About Armstrong Avenue" (part 3), Feb. 3, 2008. Den-Tex Tourist Hotel, Dr. W.C. Rutledge, Bill Waddelow, Bob Minshew, St. Vincent's Hospital in Sherman.

"Names Change But Streets Remain the Same" (part 2), Aug. 20, 2008. Booklet titled "Denison, the Texas Gateway" (1907); residents and their businesses.

"New Eisenhower Story Surfaces," Aug. 10, 2008. Lonnie S. Roberts, Jennie Jackson, birth certificate.

"One Family [Hill] Tells Their History in McKinney" (Confederate Veterans, part 3), Feb. 24, 2008. "Woot" Hill, "Tuck" Hill, Frank and Jesse James, Quantrill's Raiders, Isaac and Albert Graves, clean out bushwhackers, surrender.

"Parade Wear Fancy at Turn of the Century," Sept. 14, 2008. Labor Day parade photos, Woodmen of the World float, first tent store (Benoist & Nevins, Oct. 1872).

"Pillsbury Bake-offs Can Bring the Big Bucks," Apr. 27, 2008. Ann Pillsbury, Ballard & Ballard, Pillsbury Mills, Oscar Kollert Grocery.

"Public Works Art from '30s Still Shines Today," Nov. 2, 2008. Dr. Victoria Cummins, George D. Biddle, Paul Klepper, Jimmy Swan, Carnegie Library, murals, Red River Historical Museum/Sherman Museum.

"Railroad Museum Gets Second Chance," Mar. 5, 2008.

"Railroad Museum Going Full Steam Ahead," June 15, 2008.

"Reaching Out To Touch Someone," May 11, 2008. Two telephone companies (1886-1918), Southwestern Bell Telephone, ice storms, dial, long-distance service, cell phone.

"Red Flag Stood as Warning of Road Danger," Apr. 3, 2008. Corner of Woodard and Rusk, slow street repairs, Maude Peel Kretsinger (radio personality), Opal Dishner, Arthur P. Dishner, Jesse James, Frank James, Raymond Hamilton, beauty shop, Bonnie Parker, Clyde Barrow.

"Red River [Railroad] Museum Needs Saving," Feb. 27, 2008.

"Red River Railroad Museum Continues To Expand," Nov. 27, 2008.

"Reflections of the Katy at the Depot," July 20, 2008. *Denison Herald* special edition (13 Dec. 1987), official merger with Union Pacific (12 Aug. 1988).

"Remember When Retailers Gave Green Stamps," June 11, 2008. Drive-in theaters, drive-in restaurants, carhops, Burma Shave signs, nostalgia.

"Remembering a Part of Denison's History" (South Armstrong Avenue, part 1), Jan. 20, 2008. Highway 75, Sugar Bottom, tourist camps, filling stations.

"Remembering Aunt Polly and Her Trying Times," Mar. 12, 2008. Bill Brown, Colbert OK, Aunt Polly (former slave), plantation, food, sewing, Mrs. Bacon's store.

"Remembering Grayson County Landmarks," Oct. 8, 2008. (Items from *Denison Herald*, 25 June 1972.) Claud Easterly, MKT Railroad, John B. McDougall, Edward S. "Tex" O'Reilly, "pecan tree bank," first twins, fires, Denison Canning Factory. [NOTE: Herald Democrat archive lists as "Tidbits from the Centennial Edition," Oct. 6, 2008.]

"Remembering the Old Bush Swimming Pool in Denison" (part 1), Oct. 19, 2008. 1800 block W. Johnson St., E.F. Bush, rock quarry. [NOTE: Portions of this article are incorrect. See Oct. 29, 2008.]

"Remembering the Old Stone [Texas] Marker by the [Red] River" (part 2), July 13, 2008. Marker was near Red River Bridge on Highway 75; Grover Ditto farm; red lanterns for street repairs at corner of Main Street and Houston Avenue.

"Remembering the Spirit of Christmas," Dec. 21, 2008. Carolyn Howard, "Keep Christ in Christmas" billboards, chimes for Janet White's mother, BrooksTone Opera House.

"Remembering When: That Fateful Day in December of 1941," Dec. 7, 2008. Pearl Harbor Day.

"[S.M.] Babb Remembered for Service to the Katy," Jan. 9, 2008. Worked 48 continuous years for MKT as fireman and engineer.

"Sherman-Denison Twins Once Big in Texoma," June 25, 2008. [NOTE: Herald Democrat archives lists as "Early Denison Baseball," June 22, 2008.]

"SOSU Professor [Billie Letts] Is Successful Writer," Aug. 3, 2008.

"Stories of the Katy's Crash at Crush," Aug. 31, 2008.

"Stories of WWII from an Old Denisonian [Col. Foey Shiflet]," Mar. 16, 2008. DHS Class of 1935.

"Story Engages Local Memories of Denison History" (South Armstrong Avenue, part 2), Jan. 30, 2008. German Evangelical Church, Odd Fellows, businesses. [NOTE: Herald Democrat archive lists as "History of St. Joseph's Church."]

"The Ordinances of Days Gone By" (part 1), Oct. 1, 2008. Mortimer M. "Snake Editor" Scholl, "dress not belonging to his or her sex" outlawed, Belle Starr, McDougall Hotel.

"The Sound of 'Play Ball' Still Echoes," June 29, 2008. Early baseball teams, Railroaders. [NOTE: Herald Democrat archive lists as "Sher-Den Twins Return as Youth League Team."]

"Trains Propelled Denison's Progress," Jan. 6, 2008. First train (1872), Texas Special, celebration (1932), Patrick H. Tobin (interview).

"Whiterock [Missionary Baptist Church], First Baptist Church of Grayson County [1873]," Feb. 13, 2008. African American congregation, J.L. Luper.

"Woodmen of the World Has Rich History in Denison," Dec. 10, 2008. 201 W. Woodard St. (built 1912), fire (Mar. 1972), insurance.

2009

"A Fourth of July Snow? It Happened in 1920," July 8, 2009. Flowing Wells, Hagerman Wildlife Refuge, "Dead Woman's Pond."

"A Hero [Capt. Chesley B. Sullenberger] Comes Home," June 11, 2009. "Hometown Heroes" event (June 6). [NOTE: Listed in Herald Democrat archive as "Celebration of Heroes a Red-Letter Day for Denison," June 10, 2009.]

"A Journey on Hooves: A Local Man's [Sgt. Emmitt Roberts] Story," May 17, 2009. Mounted horse platoon in World War II. [NOTE: Listed in Herald Democrat archives as "Sergeant Roberts Rode into History in Berlin," May 19, 2009.]

"Ascertaining the Location of Flagpole Hill" (Riverside Park, part 2), June 21, 2009. Eddie Savage, Red River, Duck Creek, Munson pasture, hunting, fishing, roadside park.

"Auto Sales Has Long History in Denison," Sept. 23, 2009. Ford, Henry Pearce Auto Company (1911), Hal Collins, C.B. Middleton, Bob Giles, fire (4 July 1964). [NOTE: Herald Democrat archive lists as "The Car in Denison History."]

"Boats on the Red River and Other Memories of Denison's History," Apr. 15, 2009. Tom B. Anderson, houseboat, Red River trip, 100 block W. Main St., schools, businesses, Sugar Bottom, telephones, city limits, viaduct, fairgrounds, horse race track, "Dummy Line," "Night of Terror," R.S. Legate.

"Catching Up on Old Times, Good Friends," June 19, 2009. Sharia Ramey Nichols saved as train hit car, artist/writer Al Clymer. [NOTE: Listed in Herald Democrat archive as "Story of a Miracle."]

"Christmas Brings a Special Spirit of Giving," Dec. 23, 2009. Santa Claus stand-ins, Tedd Riffell.

"Class Rings Find Their Way Home," July 22, 2009. DHS Class of 1925, Emma Louise Baker, Lois Bilderback; Class of 1961, Karen Barnes Wilmot. [NOTE: Herald Democrat archive lists as "Ring Journey."]

"Denison Has Impressive Connections," Feb. 25, 2009. Literary agent Annie Laurie Williams, *Gone with the Wind*, Lee Malone, "The Nook" Cafe, Carl's Cafe.

"Denison Reunions Help Mark the Passage of Time," Oct. 7, 2009. DHS Class of 1953, Historic DHS clock tower, Capt. Chesley B. Sullenberger, *Highest Duty* (book). [NOTE: Herald Democrat archive lists as "Denison High School Reunions."]

"Denison Woman [Elizabeth "Betty" Phillips Foster] Recounts 101 Years," July 19, 2009. Expert dancer, shoe shop on Armstrong Avenue, nurse.

"Denison's Butane Explosion [1944] Remembered," Nov. 25, 2009. [NOTE: Herald Democrat archive lists as "Recalling Denison's Worst Disaster."]

"Denison's Distinguished Alumni Recognized," Sept. 9, 2009. Gregory T. Davis, Don Lummus, Dr. Don Russell, David Ray Smith.

"Denison's Early Labor Day Events Festive" (part 2), Sept. 11, 2009. Labor unions, "Hello Girls" (telephone operators, 1904), blacksmith, painters. [NOTE: This article duplicates one published on Sept. 8, 2009. Listed in Herald Democrat archive as "Scrapbook Helps with Historical Perspective of Labor Day."]

"Denison's Yellow Jacket Boats Had Famous Partner [Roy Rogers]" (part 1), Mar. 4, 2009.

"DHS Graduates of 1966 'Band' Together," Apr. 26, 2009. DHS Yellow Jacket Band, Capt. Chesley B. Sullenberger, Charley A. Allen, Dr. Don Brandt, Traveler's Hotel, Allen Burgh, Hwy 91, cabins.

"Discussion Concerning Denison's First Born," June 3, 2009. Denison Nelson, Texana Denison McElvany, Sam Hanna Jr., meat market, Grace Lutheran Church, Educational Institute.

"Distinguished Alumni Recognized in Denison," Oct. 23, 2009. Doak Bishop, David M. Munson, Gregory T. Davis, Philip H. Hurley.

"Duo [Donna Hord Hunt, Mavis Anne Bryant] Writes About DISD's History," May 3, 2009. *Two Schools on Main Street: The Pride of Denison, Texas, 1873–2007* (book).

"During the Time of Western Settlers," Mar. 22, 2009. Old Settlers Picnic (1879), minutes, speakings, Old Settlers Association (2009).

"Early Law Man [Lee Simmons] Helped Clean Up the Young, Brash Town of Denison" (part 1), Oct. 28, 2009. Grayson County sheriff (1912 and 1914), head of Texas Prison System.

"Everheart Family Prominent in Grayson County History," Mar. 18, 2009. Whitewright TX, Sheriff Bill Everheart, Lee-Peacock feud, first train to Denison.

"Former Navy Officers Find Friendship in Veterans' Group," Jan. 25, 2009. World War II, 40 veterans, Siras Browning, Bill McKinney, Dan Mooney, others.

"From Cartography To the Car, Maps of Main Street Show Change," Aug. 30, 2009. Sanborn's Insurance Maps (1885, 1892), various downtown blocks, comparisons to 1953 City Directory. [NOTE: Refers to articles of Aug. 2 and 19, 2009.]

"Going Back to 1950s in Denison," Aug. 19, 2009. Various downtown blocks, businesses, 1953 City Directory; lost class rings, Emma Louise Baker.

"Here, There and Everywhere on the Old [1891 Bird's-Eye] Map," Sept. 6, 2009. Cotton Mill, Exposition Hall, Educational Institute, A.R. Collins Block, National Commercial College, Security Building, State National Bank, J.J. Fairbanks House, Water Works, St. Xavier's Academy.

"In Fashion, Time Marches On As Well," Aug. 2, 2009. Businesses on Main St.

"Inventing the First Ice Cream Soda," Feb. 8, 2009. Joseph Anton Euper, confectionery, Ashburn's Creamery, Yellow Jacket Cafe (610 W. Main St.).

"It's a Small World From Where Stories Come," Oct. 11, 2009. Peabody Elementary School, Edna Mae Tones Wagner (teacher), Historic Denison High School (demolished 2007), clock tower dismantled, Billy Joe Royal DVD, Joe Pollaro, R.D. Beirne.

"Jack Maguire's Other Book," Jan. 18, 2009. *Talk of Texas, Katy's Baby.*

"Katy Gives City of Denison a Jump Start," Dec. 27, 2009. First train (Christmas, 1872), Patrick H. Tobin, Mrs. Bill Linden, Red River City. [NOTE: Listed in Herald Democrat archive as "The First Denison Christmas," Dec. 24, 2009.]

"Labor Day Once Came Before School Started" (part 1), Sept. 8, 2009. Labor unions, "Hello Girls" (telephone operators), blacksmith, painters. [NOTE: This article duplicates one from Sept. 11, 2009. Herald Democrat archive lists as "Scrapbook Helps with Historical Perspective of Labor Day."]

"Local Photographer [Rosalyn Parish] Turns Author in Golden Years," Aug. 16, 2009. Sherman TX, Parish Photo Studio, 1897 Tornado, memoirs, Wesley Village.

"Local Writer [Suzye Marino] Recounts Beginning of Career," July 26, 2009.

"Longtime Grayson Lawman [Lee Simmons] Involved in Bonnie and Clyde Case" (part 2), Nov. 1, 2009. Patti Chapman Olmstead (Simmons granddaughter).

"Looking at the Spanish-American War [1898]," Mar. 8, 2009. Troop L, First Texas Cavalry AKA Denison Rifles; Capt. Isaac N. Layne, Charles Ormsby, muster-out roll.

"Looking into the Mysteries of the Area's Past," Nov. 18, 2009. Josie Young disappeared (1967), Flagpole Hill, washboards, Willis Whitten.

"Memories Are Fond of Boats Built in Denison" (part 3), Apr. 1, 2009. Wooden Boat Association, Yellow Jacket Boats, Stinger Boats, Roy

Rogers, Elvin E. Gaines, Mia Marsico Munson, George Theakston, David Kanally, Gene Lenore, Jane Ellen Myers.

"More About Flagpole Hill and Riverside Park" (part 3), June 28, 2009. "Squirrely Bob" (hermit), Beverly Powers lost, Bud Young, campground; Carl's Restaurant, Peggy Benedict, other cafes.

"More Memories Echo from Woodmen Circle Home" (part 4), Oct. 25, 2009. Jeanie Willard, Dora Alexander Talley, Linda Robertson, membership card, Denison WOW Hall fire (1972).

"More to Say About Denisonian Killed at Pearl Harbor" (part 2), Dec. 16, 2009. Jesse L. Adams, Gold Star Mothers, books about local veterans.

"Much History Behind Storied Hopewell [Baptist] Church Location," May 6, 2009. 531 W. Bond St., Terrell Griggs Marshall Park, Augustus Terrell, A.R. Griggs, Sutton E. Griggs, Thurgood Marshall, Obie Greenleaf.

"Musician Bob Boatright" (obituary), Jan. 3, 2009. Fiddler, Texas Playboys, Horace Groff. [NOTE: Title may not be exact.]

"Mystery of Burning Hospital [St. Vincent's, Sherman TX] Solved" (part 2), Sept. 30, 2009. Judy McGraw, two fires (1988).

"Neilson Rogers and His Wit," Feb. 22, 2009. Sherman attorney, *Collected Writings*.

"Old Ironsides Has Denison Ties," Mar. 11, 2009. Martha "Queenie" Simms, John Kelley, Capt. Edmund E. Kelley, *Reindeer*, whales can talk, Dave Miller, walking.

"Old Photographs Tell Great Family Stories," Sept. 2, 2009. Lydia Raser Hendrix Snavely.

"Old Settlers Paved the Way for Much of Grayson County History," Dec. 20, 2009. Old Settlers Association, first meeting (1879), Dill's Grove, Old Settlers Park, grants.

"Once a Yellow Jacket, Always a Yellow Jacket" (part 2), Mar. 15, 2009. Elvin E. Gaines, Stinger Boat Company, world racing record (1964), Yellow Jacket Boat Company, Wyman Tamplen, Victor Brown, Victor Boats.

"One Man's [Tom B. Anderson] Account of Early Texoma History Full of Firsts," Apr. 12, 2009.

"Pearl Harbor Attack Remembered" (part 1), Dec. 7, 2009. Jesse L. Adams, DHS Class of 1942, Dr. Dorothy Hawkins Rushing, troop trains, Glenna Brigham McConnell.

"Population Ups and Downs," Feb. 3, 2009 (part 2). Population figures, number of dwellings, businesses, growth after 1872, Marvin Springer's comprehensive plan (1964), census. [NOTE: From Herald Democrat archive. Printed title and date may differ slightly.]

"Potato Wars on Board the *USS O'Bannon*," Jan. 25, 2009. [NOTE: Sidebar to article titled "Former Navy Officers Find Friendship in Veterans' Group."]

"Railroad Big in Denison Heritage," Mar. 25, 2009. Grand reopening, Red River Railroad Museum, Union Pacific's "Katy Heritage 1988" locomotive, train simulator, films.

"Readers Share Memories of Denison," Nov. 11, 2009. "I Remember When" columns (1986), W.M. Bradbury, military, cavalry, Denison Dam, POW camp, Bessie Yowell, crossing Red River, first peanut thresher, Mrs. W.O. Weaver, roads, Gray Field (airport), R.M. "Dick" Gray, bus service on Ambrose Road, Kraft Cheese route.

"Recollections of Riverside Park in Denison" (part 1), June 14, 2009. Red River, W.B. Munson, *Annie P*, Colbert's Ferry, Dago Hill, Oakwood Cemetery, Flagpole Hill, hermit, roads, toll bridge, map. [NOTE: Listed in Herald Democrat archive as "Where Is Riverside Park?" June 12, 2009.]

"Remembering Her Historical Visit: Former First Lady Eleanor Roosevelt Visits Durant, Oklahoma," Mar. 29, 2009.

"Remembering Legendary Law Men," Oct. 4, 2009. Jesse L. "Red" Hall, Skiddy Street, Anna Belle Powell Barrow Medford Turner (gang leader), police force, Clarence Faecke.

"Remembering St. Vincent's Sanitarium [Sherman TX]" (part 1), Sept. 27, 2009. Fire (1988).

"Remembering the Early Autos of Texoma," May 21, 2009. Max S. Lale, Elmer E. Davis, stable fire (13 Dec. 1908), car wreck, street commissioner, parade for Davis (1916).

"Remembering the House [William T.] Lankford Built," June 7, 2009. Riverside Park.

"Report of UFO Over Perrin in 1953 Now Declassified," Aug. 23, 2009.

"Sherman's Wild and Wooly Days Gone By," Dec. 6, 2009. James Henry Dillon, first Frisco train, drug stores, bootleggers, saloons, Neilson Rogers, Mary Fitch, G.A. Dickerman.

"Sherman's Woodmen Circle Home Cared for Orphans" (part 2), Oct. 18, 2009. [NOTE: Herald Democrat archive lists as "Life in the Woodmen Circle Home."]

"Something About That Carl's Cafe," May 10, 2009. Citizens National Bank expansion, 112 N. Rusk Ave., Peggy Benedict, "Jew" Benedict, Denison Food Store, other businesses dislocated, Ricki Rollins, Cashion schools.

"Story of Woodmen Circle Home Unfolds" (part 1), Oct. 14, 2009.

"Texoma Loses a Distinguished Military Hero," Feb. 15, 2009. [NOTE: Herald Democrat archive lists as "Buddy Wagner Made Denison Proud."]

"The Blue Plate at the Eat-Well Cafe" (part 2), Feb. 18, 2009. Mary Vick, Ruth Tignor, Carl McCraw, other cafes, Christman's Bakery, Dr. C.B. Sullenberger, sailplanes.

"The Cafes of Yesterday Live in Lore" (part 1), Feb. 1, 2009. O.K. Restaurant, Eat-Well, Green Gables, Saratoga, Tom-Tom, White Pig, others.

"The Famous Bugle and the Man [Hartley B. Edwards] That Played It," July 12, 2009. End of World War I, Gen. John J. Pershing, Smithsonian Institution, Perrin AFB Museum.

"The Old West and the Silver Screen," Aug. 9, 2009. Billy Holcomb, Gene Autry, Hopalong Cassidy, cowboys, music, poetry.

"The Ups and Downs of Growing Small Towns" (part 1), Jan. 28, 2009. Denison's growth in first year, boom in 1880s, businesses in 1895.

"They're Leaving a Legacy for Grayson County," Mar. 1, 2009. Black History Month, Dr. Claude Organ Jr., Clora Bryant, Marguerite Bradshaw, JoAnn Perkins.

"This Subject Will Have You Wrapped Around Its Finger," Aug. 12, 2009. DHS class rings, TPW pin, Loi-Mac Pharmacy named for Lois Bilderback.

"Treasures Found Among Sale Items," July 16, 2009.

"Up, Up and Away Over Denison," Aug. 26, 2009. Hot-air balloon ascensions: Woodlake (1906), Chet Baldwin, Mrs. Fred Luck; Exposition Hall; recent.

"Ups and Downs of a Growing Town [Denison]" (part 3), Feb. 5, 2009. Saloons, proprietors, other businesses, newspapers, 1876-77 City Directory.

"Viaduct Long a Central Artery to Downtown Denison," Nov. 8, 2009. Three earlier viaducts (early 1880s, 1915, 1954), new one (2013). [NOTE: Herald Democrat archive lists as "History of the Denison Viaduct" and "Katy Car Shops."]

"Visitor [David Schroth] Shares Memories of Denison [1958–63]," June 24, 2009. Lawrence Zika, MKT Railroad.

"Woodmen Circle Home Passes To Other Owners" (part 3), Oct. 21, 2009.

2010

"A Bonnie Parker Attended Stevens School in Denison," Sept. 9, 2010. Louise Roberts Dobbins, Ida Shreves (principal), Principal's Annual Register (1900-1907), teachers.

"Article Listing Col. John Potts Was Correct," Dec. 19, 2010. Preston Bend, William C. Quantrill, James A. Potts (founded Pottsboro TX), James G. Thompson, George Butt.

"Big Events Unfolding Can Cause Presses to Hold," Jan. 27, 2010. Kennedy assassination, Beall's fire (24 Dec. 1989), Vietnamese bus crash (8 Aug. 2008), "Hometown Heroes" event (Capt. Chesley B. Sullenberger, 2 June 2009), "Caddo Shootout" (1978), prison escape, manhunt, deaths.

"Book Recounts Colorful History of Grayson County," Feb. 17, 2010. Mattie Davis Lucas, Mita Holsapple Hall, book (1936), now on Portal to Texas History.

"[Bredette C.] Thomas Highest Flying Denison High School Graduate [Class of 1960]" (part 1), Apr. 11, 2010. Test pilot, Blackbird fighter jet, B.C. Murray, Mayor L.S. Owings.

"Bristol Palin Gets Raw Deal from Ladies on 'The View'" (Mineral Wells TX, part 1), Nov. 21, 2010. Hal Collins, Dave Blackburn, Crazy Waters Crystal Company, Texas Quality Network, FDA fines.

"Carpenter's [Bluff] Bridge, 8 Miles East of Denison for 100 Years," June 13, 2010. "Texas' back door," Earl Elijah Carpenter, Red River, ferry crossing, Flood of 1908, bridge built 1910, Kathryn Plunkett, MO&G Railroad, Dr. Clyde Hall.

"Crape Myrtles Prominent Through History in Denison," Aug. 1, 2010. Jennie Jackson, mass planting (1938); Edward F. O'Herin, MKT Railroad; Riverside School; street railway system (authorized 1883); Gate City Business College (1884), Harshaw, "Golden Rule" rulers.

"Dallas Man Brings Back Yellow Jacket Boat," May 5, 2010. Wooden Boat Association, Chuck Pool, David Kanally, William Collins Bauder, restoration; Historic DHS, statues, DHS Alumni Association minutes (1909–19); Alamo painting, Bailey Drug Store; Justin Raynal's Monument.

"Denison Boys Volunteered for Military Service in 1917" (part 1), July 11, 2010. World War I, Dean Burget, Charles Harris, Kingston's Drug Store; send-offs, Katy Brass Band; volunteer groups: (1) 45 (list) under Dr. J.G. Ellis Jr., field hospital work; (2) 55 (list) under Leo J. Waltz, U.S. Army.

"Denison Graduates, Athletes To Be Recognized," Sept. 26, 2010. Denison Alumni Association, Distinguished Alumni, Carl E. Bilderback, Jerome L. "Jerry" Duggan, Jim Hightower, Emily C. Jones, Drewey D. McKnight Jr., Joseph "Joe" Duggan, Fred A. Taylor.

"Denison Has Long History of Producing Musicians," Nov. 7, 2010. Phil McDade, Brownsville community, Iron Ore Baptist Church, Rose

Pleasant, Anna L. Green, Columbus OH, Clora Bryant, Helen Cole, Marva Lewis, Marguerite Bradshaw.

"Denison History Included in 'Documenting the American South'" (part 1), Apr. 4, 2010. Edward King, James Wells Champney, illustrations. [NOTE: Original publication was *The Great South; A Record of Journeys in Louisiana, Texas, the Indian Territory, Missouri....* (Hartford, CN: American Publishing Co., 1875). Full facsimile online.]

"Denison History Unfolds in Copies of Old Newspapers," Nov. 17, 2010. *Sunday Gazetteer* (2 Dec. 1900), soap factory, macaroni factory, George Moulton, asphalt, Henry Heath, yams, streetlights; *Gazetteer* (20 Dec. 1925), football, Hal Collins, Dave Blackburn, hunting trip, timber wolf.

"Denison Pioneers Lived Rich, Long Lives," Feb. 10, 2010. Lou Harris (interview, 11 June 1936), oldest woman in Grayson County, four wars, musician; Helen A. Morrison Cummins (second oldest); pianist Newell Cummins; Mrs. Bill Linden.

"Denison Set the Bar for Road Repairs in 1907," May 19, 2010. T.W. Larkin, Board of Trade, jail inmates, farmers, businessmen, Carpenter's Bluff road. [NOTE: Herald Democrat archive lists as "In 1907, Road Construction Made National News."]

"Denison Was the Location of the First Union Depot in Texas," Oct. 4, 2010. Fire (first depot, 15 Mar. 1874), second depot joint project of MK&T and H&TC, McDougall Hotel, third depot (1914).

"Denison-Owned Yellow Jacket Boat in Dallas Boat Show," Feb. 7, 2010. Chuck Pool, Merle Bullock, Roy Rogers, Clifton McDerby, Keith Hubbard, "French Avenue gang."

"Denison's Early Years Intertwine with Chinese Pioneers," Mar. 30, 2010. Oakwood Cemetery, Dr. Lawrence A. Washington, Chinese tombstone, Dr. Lloyd W.C. Tang, Chinese laundries, B.M. "Beverly" Steele, John W. Green, Dr. Alex W. Acheson, veterans.

"Denisonians Gather for Annual Reunion—in California," July 25, 2010. Ethel Thorne recalls Dr. Alexander W. Acheson.

"Denisonians Have Ties to Colorado Getaway," Jan. 8, 2010. Rod and Gun Club, Creede CO, old guest register, Hortense Lingo (Mrs. Willard) Burton, J.J. Fairbanks, A.F. Platter, Chautauqua. [NOTE: Herald Democrat archive lists as "Early Denison Clubs."]

"Early Denison Seen Through the Eyes of 1873 Visitors" (part 2), Apr. 7, 2010. Edward King, James Wells Champney, Robert Benecke, *Scribner's Monthly*, Sherman TX.

"Famous Denison Native Tex O'Reilly Remained Largely Unknown in His Hometown," Mar. 17, 2010. Texas Nursery, Sam Roy; Jack R. Maguire; soldier of fortune, Dr. Alexander W. Acheson.

"Fannin County Museum Links Heritage to Local Pioneer Family," Jan. 13, 2010. William W. Russell, Annie Russell Bradford, Claude Bradford, Bradford House, furnishings.

"Full Details of the Vin Fiz Adventure Revealed," Mar. 14, 2010. Calbraith P. Rogers, first airplane to fly over Denison (1911), landed in Judge Jim Bryant's pasture, Smithsonian Institution.

"Gladys Riddle [Mrs. Lionel Hampton] Among the Famous from Denison," Oct. 20, 2010. J.H. Riddle family, Dr. Roscoe C. Riddle, Hollywood, Clora Bryant, Jim Sears.

"Graveside Ceremony Held for Man [Col. Benjamin F. Carter] Whose Last Wish Was for Christian Burial" (part 2), June 23, 2010. Sons of Confederate Veterans, Steve Hutchison, ceremonies in PA and Austin TX.

"Grayson County History Celebrated in Two Events," Sept. 29, 2010. Orphan Trains, Woodmen Circle Home, David McNees (owner), Red River Historical Museum/Sherman Museum.

"Happiness Comes from Inside All of Us," Dec. 26, 2010. Bill Brown, Harless Memorial UMC, Grandma Cooper, Grandma Brown, wildflowers on Grandpa's grave.

"Historic Denison Building [Waples-Platter Grocery, 1874] Will Be Closed a While Longer," July 4, 2010. MK&T Railroad Offices, Katy Antique Station, damaged corner; Sam Hanna, Joe Owens, Andrew F. Platter, Edward H. Lingo, Edward B. Waples, Paul Waples, John Waples, Pierre Lelardoux (architect).

"Information for Historical Markers Being Gathered," May 9, 2010. Donald Mayes House, Waples Memorial Methodist Church, Sadler Cemetery, Martindale-Lackey-Hudgins Cottage (Whitewright), Pool Cemetery near Texoma Medical Center.

"Judge [R.C.] Vaughan Also Called 'Unkie'" (obituary), Mar. 21, 2010.

"Keeping Memorabilia Helps Keep History Alive," Sept. 15, 2010. Schools (Stevens, Raynal, Central Ward, Burleson), ward system; Sam Rayburn, S.R. Melugin, W.B. "Willie" Head, Janet Francis, Savoy TX, cardboard camera; G.A. Dickerman, Danna Dickerman Conaway.

"Lawmen End Notorious Gangster Era," Mar. 10, 2010. Clyde Barrow's sister Artie lived in Denison (had Cinderella Beauty Shoppe, 430 W. Sears St.), Robert C. Elston, reenactments. [NOTE: Listed in Herald Democrat archive as "1934 Not a Good Year for Gangsters," Mar. 9, 2010.]

"Local Community Supporter, [Ray] Clymer, Passes at Age 85" (obituary), June 24, 2010. [NOTE: Herald Democrat archive lists as "One of TMC's Pioneers, Ray Clymer, Dies in Wichita Falls."]

"Location of First Grayson County Court Identified," Feb. 24, 2010. *Denison Herald* (17 Mar. 1946, 12 Aug. 1978), Robert Atchison, Iron Ore Creek, Dr. Morris Britton, W.H. "Hank" McLain, Lucinda Jane Atchison (first white child born in Grayson County), Joseph Mitchell, ferry, Holland Coffee, Charles A. Galloway, Shawnee Trail, Bonehead Club.

"Looking Back on 2010 As It Comes To an End," Dec. 29, 2010. Jim Sears, "flopped" yearbook photos, Capt. Chesley B. Sullenberger, Joe Cole's doorknob, Hawkins' traveling rooster, DHS Alumni Association minutes (1909-1919), Mosse women (teachers), Kim Hayes Hardy in Haiti, Carpenter's Bluff, Woodmen's Circle Home, B.C. Thomas (test pilot).

"Looking Back on the Local History in 2009 and Beyond," Jan. 1, 2010. Fiddler Bob Boatright (obituary), Jack Maguire, Navy vets, small towns, Joseph A. Euper, "Sully" Sullenberger, class rings, Buddy Wagner (obituary), Yellow Jacket Boats, Eleanor Roosevelt visited Durant OK, Truman Wester (obituary), Flagpole Hill, snow on July 4, bugler Hartley Edwards, writer Suzye Marino, Woodmen Circle Home, gangsters, viaduct, Pearl Harbor, *Two Schools on Main Street* (book).

"Many Firsts Took Place in Denison's Early Days," Oct. 17, 2010. Educational Institute, Red River navigation, *Annie P*, Preston Trail, Red River City, railroads, Interurban, Forest Park, paved road, ice cream soda, first court session, post office, Theodore Roosevelt visit, Vin Fiz.

"Mayor [W.S.] Hibbard's Impact on Denison Chronicled by Wife [Sue Newby Hibbard]," Aug. 8, 2010. Mercy Hospital dedication, police, Southwestern Bell Telephone Company, jelly bean contest.

"Mineral Waters Flowed Through Grayson County," Nov. 28, 2010. Tioga TX, Gene Autry, fire (1947); Jacobs Hotel and Resort, Milo Jacobs.

"Mystery Continues to Surround Names of Area Towns" (part 2), May 30, 2010. Van Alstyne, Anna, Melissa, Cherry Mound, Carpenter's Bluff, Smith Oaks (R.E.L. Smith).

"Origins of Towns' Names Can Be Interesting, Mysterious" (part 1), May 23, 2010. Ambrose Bible, Riverside Confectionery, Melissa, more.

"Pearl Harbor Attack Is Still Remembered," Dec. 7, 2010. Jesse L. Adams family, Roy Nichols, Allen Allender, Frank Graves.

"Pecan Harvesting Changed from Years Past," Jan. 20, 2010. Cherry Mound, Bill Crabtree.

"Pictures Were 'Flopped' Even in the Old Days," Feb. 28, 2010. DHS *Yellow Jacket* (yearbook), Class of 1969, Jim Sears, Capt. Chesley B. "Sully" Sullenberger, Kay Casey (teacher).

"Pink Hill Community Predates Denison," May 2, 2010. Apr. 2002 (two columns), name, Washburns, Houstons, Dugans, Indians; Post Office Drug Store, Rusk Avenue, Anne Rowland, Edna Davis, ice storm (1945), Loi-Mac Pharmacy.

"Population in Area Has Had Ups and Downs Through the Years," Feb. 3, 2010.

"President Eisenhower Visited Denison in '46, '52, '65" (part 1), Oct. 27, 2010. Campaigning, naming Eisenhower Auditorium.

"Presidents Came to Perrin for Sam Rayburn's Funeral" (part 3), Nov. 10, 2010. James Gattis, lunch with JFK in Germany; Rayburn's death (16 Nov. 1961), Presidents Johnson, Truman, Eisenhower; City Market (14 Apr. 1873), Educational Institute, Charles Wheelock, W.G. Melville.

"Rambling Rooster Rides to Waco and Back," May 16, 2010. Tom and Pauline Hawkins; Pink Hill Baptist Church, Saphronia Houston Reynolds. [NOTE: Herald Democrat archive lists as "Traveling Rooster."]

"Ranch Style Beans Started in Denison," Apr. 25, 2010. Waples-Platter Grocery Company, Sam Hanna, Joe Owens, commissary, coffee, Lloyd McKee, Great Western Foods, A.F. Platter, MKT Office Building, Katy Antique Station.

"Readers Add Information About Some Past Columns," Apr. 28, 2010. DHS Alumni Association, minutes (1909-1919), Mosse women (teachers), Historic DHS cornerstone lost, Sarah Burleson (lawyer in New York City).

"Recent Extreme Weather Not the First for Texoma Area," Jan. 11, 2010. July 4 snow, Flowing Wells, hail storm (1925), D.J. Bell electrocuted, Green Wilson drowning, Kingston's Drug thermometer, record temperatures (1930), ice storm (1945), fires.

"Relics of Days Gone By Offer Glimpse of History," Aug. 11, 2010. Palace Hotel, hotel register (1915–20), Thompson's Drug Store, J.M. Crumpton, Arthur O. Simpson, Hotel Denison (1924).

"Remembering Jazz Musician [Booker T.] Ervin and Christmases Past," Dec. 12, 2010.

"Remembering the Social Life in Early Denison," Aug. 22, 2010. WCTU, Denison Philosophical and Social Club, McDougall Opera House, churches, Verein Vorwaerts, Presbyterian Church bell (1876), Sisters of St. Mary of Namur buy Ed Perry house (1876), St. Xavier's Academy dedication (1901), Lon McAleer, Sugar Bottom, orphan.

"Sage Advice of 1953 Applies Today," Sept. 19, 2010. DHS Class of 1953, student directory, Willis A. Sutton (graduation speaker).

"Scrapbook in Lubbock Junk Yard Has Information for DHS Class of 1926," Nov. 3, 2010. Rita Massey, teachers, Woodlake, Baer's Ferry, statue of doughboy, TCU.

"Southwest 'Bad Guys' Lived as Respectable Denison Citizens," July 8, 2010. W.E. Koop, Wichita KS, "Rowdy Joe" Lowe, "Rowdy Kate," "Saloon Massacre" (Newton KS), Rock Jack Norton.

"Story of Boneheads in Denison Was Told by *Denison Herald* Editor Claud Easterly," Feb. 21, 2010. Bonehead Club of Dallas, Denison Lions Club, MK&T Railroad officials, pranks.

"Story of Confederate Soldier [Col. Benjamin F. Carter] Complicated, but Interesting" (part 1), June 20, 2010. A.C. Bailey, Alexander K. McClure, Dr. Abraham Senseney, burials, Chambersburg PA.

"Technology Is Both a Blessing and Curse" (B.C. Thomas, part 2), Apr. 14, 2010. Lost photos.

"[Ted] Pylant Tells Story About Shooting in Denison in the 1880s," July 18, 2010. Joseph Blagg, incident (*Sunday Gazetteer*, 1 Sept. 1889), C.H. Scholl, *Evening Dispatch*.

"Texas, Oklahoma Keep Culture Alive Through Language," Aug. 25, 2010. Town names, old sayings.

"The Cotton Compress Among Denison's Rich Business History," Mar. 24, 2010. Patrick H. Tobin, M.A. Joy, new building (1926), Horace Ash, H.W. Green, landscaping.

"The Denison Boys of WWI Remembered" (part 2), July 14, 2010. Dr. J.G. Ellis Jr., Guy Cox, Ambulance Company No. 27, casualties, Mart Coppin, Fred William Wilson Jr., American Legion, Collie D. Henson, Dean Burget, Denison Canteen (photo).

"The Door Knob a Tie to the Past," Sept. 5, 2010. [NOTE: Herald Democrat archive lists as "Joe Cole's Door Knob."]

"Today's Treasures Turn Out To Be Yesterday's News," June 16, 2010. Lucious R. Hord, Judge R.C. Vaughan, "The [Denison] Herald's Letter to Servicemen" (1 Nov. 1943), news digest, Tropical Gardens, nightclub, Halloween party, Carl McCraw, Kenneth Mills, Carpenter's Bluff, Red River bridges, First Baptist Church, chickens.

"Turn-of-the-Century Visitor's Guide Shows Snapshot of Life in 1899," May 26, 2010. U.S. Post Office (built 1908–1912), Charles W. Nelson, William J. Scott, W.M. Nagle, Denison Post Office Guide (1899), businesses, telephones, mail carried by railroads, Parcel Post Rural Route Directory (1914), Gay-Ola soft drinks.

"'Uncle George' [G.A. Dickerman] Tells About Sherman in the Old Days," Sept. 12, 2010. Log courthouse, Col. W.C. "Bill" Young, R.R. McIntire, money.

"Veterans' Monument Coming to Denison," Apr. 18, 2010. Dwight D. Eisenhower, bust, David Adickes, Loy Lake Park, Doug Coleman, Grayson County Frontier Village, John Munson, Ben Munson III, bricks (veterans and non-veterans).

"Visits by Eisenhower Are Recalled" (part 2), Oct. 31, 2010. Bill Duckworth, Myron Thornton, Karotkin photo with Ike, Sam Rayburn of Bonham TX, Denison Dam.

"Well Water Near Mineral Wells Said to Have Healing Properties" (part 2), Nov. 24, 2010. Hal Collins, Crazy Water Crystals, Crazy Hotel, celebrities, Mineral Wells TX, Ednaville TX (1881).

"What Looks Like Trash Could Turn Out To Be a Treasure," Apr. 21, 2010. DHS Alumni Association, minutes (1909–1919), Mosse women (teachers), XXI Club, annual meetings, officers, statues, new high school (1914). [NOTE: Herald Democrat archive lists as "Denison Alumni Association 1909 Minutes Found by District Employee."]

"Yellow Jacket Boat [1956 Catalina] Turns into Show Boat," June 30, 2010. Main Street Lumber Company, Chuck Pool, Wooden Boat Association, R.A. McDerby, William Collins "Bill" Bauder, David Kanally, boat restoration, Gene Ramey, David Gill, E.E. Gaines, Stinger Boats, W.D. Collins Bank Fixture Company, Franklin Pillsbury.

2011

"1895 Post Office Guide Reveals Treasured Denison Information," Sept. 29, 2011.

"21 Historic Springs of Grayson County Would Be Great Today," Aug. 24, 2011. Gunnar Brune, *Springs of Texas* (book).

"Cemeteries [Bloomfield, Shannon] Help Tell Our Stories, History" (part 4), Aug. 21, 2011.

"Decisions About Denison Dam Affect History," Nov. 27, 2011. Grave removal, towns inundated (1944).

"Denison Firsts: Free Graded Public School [1873]" (Denison Firsts, part 6), Apr. 20, 2011.

"Denison Gets New Post Office in 1910" (Denison Firsts, part 1), Mar. 30, 2011. [NOTE: Herald Democrat archive lists as "Denison Firsts: Free Rural Mail."]

"Denison Gremlins Baseball Team Remembered [1945]," Jan. 30, 2011. [NOTE: Team members' names given in article of Feb. 6, 2011.]

"Denison History Up in Circa 1920s Catalog," July 6, 2011. Mary Maude Farms, 2110 S. Armstrong Ave.

"Denison Man [Joseph A. Euper] Creates First Ice Cream Soda" (Denison Firsts, part 2), Apr. 3, 2011.

"Denison Native [Eddy G. Nicholson] Became Top Americana Collector" (obituary), Aug. 7, 2011.

"Denison Remembers Its First Mayor, L.S. Owings" (Denison Firsts, part 4), Apr. 13, 2011.

"Denison's First Christmas Tied to Railroad History" (part 1), Dec. 21, 2011. Patrick H. Tobin.

"Doodlebugs [Budd Car] Played Important Role in Railroad History" (Little Local Railroads, part 3), Jan. 26, 2011.

"Early Denison Settlers Use Creative Ways to Battle Summer Heat," July 20, 2011. Ice cream, baseball, Woodlake, *Souvenir of Denison the Gate City* (1887), property prices.

"Early News Stories Give Insight into Denison's Past," Mar. 9, 2011. *Sunday Gazetteer* (1876, 1926), dwarfs, oil spring, fire, basketball, pecan trees, electricity.

"Famed Composer of Military Marches, Sousa, Visited Denison [Twice]," Nov. 16, 2011. Historic DHS Auditorium, YMCA.

"Famed Literary Agent [Annie Laurie Williams] from Denison," July 17, 2011. *Gone With the Wind*.

"Family Research Pays Off in Big Ways," Feb. 6, 2011. Carpenters Bluff Baseball Club (1915), Denison Gremlins Baseball Team, Arthur Henry.

"Former Denisonian [Richard Franklin] Honored by CIAA [Central Intercollegiate Athletic Association]," Jan. 23, 2011. Michael Quinn Sullivan, Lennie Tritico, Perrin AFB Band, Doodlebug trains, KO&G Railroad.

"Getting Ready To Mark Eisenhower Birthday" ("Under the Colors," *Denison Herald*, Labor Day 1943, part 1), Oct. 5, 2011. Military men and women, Richard Robinson.

"Golden Rule Students, Teachers Share Memories, Company," Aug. 10, 2011. Cotton Mill community, school built 1922, Viola Everett Brice.

"Heroism of D-Day and Veterans Remembered," June 8, 2011. Dwight D. Eisenhower, Johnny Goldston.

"It Was a Week We All Remember," Nov. 20, 2011. Assassination of John F. Kennedy.

"Items From the Mail Bag Spark More Columns," Aug. 31, 2011. Robert Leach, Interurban, Joe Espinosa's tamales, Alvin Tignor, service stations, Overland Stage, "Rock Hill Special" (song), Lionel Hampton, Gladys Riddle Hampton, Marshal Royal.

"July 4, 1879, Incident Was Amazing Story," July 3, 2011. Parade, exhibits, four killed.

"Katy Engineer Pat [Patrick H.] Tobin Brought Denison's First Ice House" (Denison Firsts, part 3), Apr. 7, 2011. Crystal Ice Company.

"Looking Back on [Rural] Grayson County School Buildings," Oct. 26, 2011. Mae Hughes.

"Looking Back on Some of Sherman's Early Days," May 22, 2011. G.A. Dickerman (1909).

"Loy Park Shows History in Beginning, Improvements," Nov. 13, 2011.

"Memories from the Day President [John F.] Kennedy Was Shot," Nov. 24, 2011.

"Miniature Train Conjures Big Memories" (Little Local Railroads, part 5), Mar. 6, 2011. James Redmon Sr., 731 W. Crawford St.

"More Denison Firsts" (Denison Firsts, part 5), Apr. 16, 2011. B.C. Murray, newspapers.

"More Information Discovered on Denison's Riverside School [and Reasor School]" (part 2), June 26, 2011. Mildred Young Lamoreaux, M.B. Thornton, Sadie Ball Swift, Denison Dam.

"Navy Veterans Remember *USS Grayson*," Dec. 18, 2011. World War II, Dan Mooney, Jerry Peddicord, kangaroo heist.

"Prostitutes a Source of Denison City Income—in 1873," Nov. 30, 2011. Early city ordinances, John Crawford, Rev. H. Daniel Morgan.

"Questions Asked About Shannon Cemetery" (part 2), June 5, 2011. Two Shannon cemeteries, James B. Shannon; early Sherman cemeteries, G.A. Dickerman.

"Railroad Deals 1922 Blow to Denison Economy," Dec. 7, 2011. Railroad Strike of 1922, Col. Charles W. Nimon, Katy Car Shops.

"Recalling Death of President [John F.] Kennedy," Nov. 20, 2011.

"Recalling Grayson County Hay Balers," Sept. 18, 2011. Fred Muller, Lawson Lafayette Holder, Red River Flood (1908), Cold Springs School.

"Remembering Days Gone By at the Pump," July 13, 2011. Filling stations, gas rationing, McKee Brothers Service Station.

"Remembering Denison Trains of Christmases Past" (part 2), Dec. 25, 2011. Patrick H. Tobin (interview), Satanta, Big Tree.

"Remembering the Hive [Youth Center] in Denison," Dec. 4, 2011.

"Remembering Those Five-and-Ten-Cent Stores," Sept. 25, 2011. J.J. Newberry, S.H. Kress (1909–1974), Wacker's, Myles Variety.

"Riverside School Removed to Make Way for Denison Dam Spillway" (part 1), June 14, 2011. Riverside Park, Riverside community, Red River, puzzle.

"Service Men and Women Remembered from Newspaper Clipping" ("Under the Colors," *Denison Herald*, Labor Day 1943, part 2), Oct. 9, 2011. Military men and women.

"Shannon Cemetery Pre-Dated Town of Denison" (part 1), May 29, 2011.

"Shortest Railroad Around Remembered" (Little Local Railroads, part 4), Feb. 27, 2011. Morton, Maurice & Baer's Ferry Railroad; Dwight D. Eisenhower; Lee's Cafe (212 W. Main St.).

"Sinking of the *Sultana* [1865] Predates the *Titanic* Tragedy," Oct. 19, 2011. Mississippi River, Irene Edwards, C.M. Eldredge (interviewed by Claud Easterly, 1940).

"Snow in July and Texoma Weather Extremes," July 24, 2011. Flowing Wells, William Pearson, heat records, keeping cool.

"Story of Terry Leonard" (part 2), May 17, 2011. Former *Denison Herald* staffer. [NOTE: Title not exact.]

"Tales of Rock Bluff Ferry [on Red River] Retold," Oct. 30, 2011. John Malcolm, wedding.

"The 'Dinkey,' Small in Stature But Mighty in Strength" (Little Local Railroads, part 2), Jan. 16, 2011. Spanish mules, "dummy line," electric streetcars, Engine No. 787, roustabout, Dinkey to Bloomfield Academy OK, routes.

"The History of Pottsboro and Its Name," Mar. 2, 2011. James Archer Potts, Judge James G. Thompson.

"The Launching of Earl J. Miller's 55-Foot Boat [*The Viola*, 1945]" (Lake Texoma boats, part 2), Sept. 7, 2011. U.S. Corps of Engineers, *The Moulton* (73-foot boat), George D. Moulton.

"The 'Nellie' [Denison, Bonham & New Orleans] Railroad Part of Life for Denison Workers" (Little Local Railroads, part 1), Jan. 12, 2011. Other small railroads (list).

"Traveling Across Country Began by Stage," May 15, 2011. Overland Mail, Waterman L. Ormsby, tips for stagecoach travel, timetables, routes.

"Two Shannon Cemeteries Exist in Grayson County" (part 3), June 12, 2011. Sarah Dye.

"U.S. Presidents Visit Denison, Texoma Area," May 11, 2011. Ulysses S. Grant, Theodore Roosevelt (1905), Franklin D. Roosevelt, Harry S. Truman, Sam Rayburn's funeral.

"Update on Denison Miniature and Original Locomotives" (Little Local Railroads, part 6), Mar. 16, 2011. James Redmon Sr. built two trains; Nellie, Ambrose TX.

"We Have Had Worse Winters," Feb. 9, 2011. Blizzard of 1899, record cold (1930), ice storms (1945, 1949). [NOTE: Herald Democrat archive lists as "Weather, 1899."]

"Website Is Treasure Trove of Information" (Lake Texoma boats, part 1), July 31, 2011. U.S. Corps of Engineers, 1945 events, *The Moulton* (boat), Higgins Boats, R.A. McDerby, Yellow Jacket Boats.

"When [Dwight D.] Eisenhower Visited Birth Place [21 Apr. 1946]," Oct. 12, 2011. Charles "Hoke" Johnson, Bobby Cloud, parade.

"Whereabouts of Former Reporter [Terry Leonard] Sought" (part 1), May 8, 2011. Gene Lenore, Denison Dam documentary, novelist Sylvia Dickey Smith.

"Woman [Tonda Kidd Crenshaw] Born During Ice Storm of 1949," Feb. 13, 2011. Calera OK, Sterrett OK, Bill Brown, Thomas L. Cooper.

"XXI Club Was Cultural Organization Formed in 1890" (Denison Firsts, part 7), Apr. 24, 2011.

2012

"70 Years Since Jimmy Doolittle's Raid on Japan" (part 1), Apr. 18, 2012. Local people involved.

"A Brief History of the Waples-Platter, Griffin, MKT, Katy Building," Dec. 2, 2012. Location: 104 East Main Street.

"A Look Back at the Griffin Peanut Company," May 31, 2012. Jeanne Newton, Charles Perry Newton (photographer); World War II, Harlon Block, Iwo Jima Memorial, Bud Roach, Celeste TX.

"A Stop at Denison's Farmers Market Brings Back Memories," May 16, 2012. Trade grounds, 100 block W. Woodard St., Patti, Zenthoefer.

"Ambrose [Texas] Was Once a Thriving Community" (part 1), June 17, 2012. Ambrose Bible, Denison Bonham & New Orleans (DB&NO) Railroad.

"Clippings of Past Elections [1952, 1912] Found," Oct. 21, 2012. Dwight D. Eisenhower, Sam Rayburn; Kyler triplets.

"Clippings Show Denison Roots," Apr. 1, 2012. Circus tragedy in Sherman TX, Liberty Bell visit, naming Dad and Lad's, Citizens National Bank, Texas stone marker, Centennial plates, DHS Class of 1925, Claud Easterly, teachers.

"Culture on Stage a Part of Early Denison," Aug. 26, 2012. Vorwaerts Society, celebrations, July 4, baseball, opera houses, movie houses.

"Davy Crockett and His Ties to Grayson County," Dec. 9, 2012. Guns exchanged (1835), Andrew Thomas, Dugans, Washburns, Daughertys.

"Denison Alumni Association to Honor Five Graduates," Oct. 15, 2012. Dr. Henry Scott, Jeff B. Powell, Dr. Rashona Thomas, Raymond Lee Hicks, Edward N. Hicks.

"Denison Fire Department Started in 1875," July 27, 2012.

"Denison First Presbyterian [Church] Marks [140th] Anniversary," Dec. 16, 2012.

"Denison Women's Christian Temperance Union in the Beginning," Aug. 15, 2012. Sarah C. Acheson, Mary Elizabeth Lease.

"Denison's Alamo Hotel Celebrated in 1873," Mar. 11, 2012. Other hotels and saloons, too.

"Denison's Gold Rush Remembered," Mar. 21, 2012. Walker Hunt farm, legends; Alamo Hotel, Henry Merrick.

"Doolittle Raid Participant [John A. Hilger] from Sherman" (part 2), Apr. 29, 2012. Bill Longley (outlaw).

"Happenings of Grayson County Before 1872" (Chronology, part 1), Dec. 5, 2012. Andrew Thomas. [Events from 1750 to 1861.]

"Historic [Rialto] Theater in Denison Still Offers Events," Oct. 17, 2012.

"Independence Day in 1847," July 4, 2012. Methodist camp meeting (1847), picnic at Courthouse Square; snow at Flowing Wells (1920).

"Information on Pioneers Found in Old Newspaper [Dated Jan. 1, 1879]," June 10, 2012. Sheriff W.C. Everheart, William B. Boss, Justin Raynal, Dr. C.B. Berry, M.H. Sherburne, Maj. R.M. Grubbs, Robert C. Foster, William Hardwick, A.H. Coffin, C.C. Schmucker, J.P. Woodyard.

"Interurban Began as Transportation Between Denison, Sherman," Mar. 18, 2012. Denison "firsts," J.P. Crear, Woodlake, Texas Electric Railway Company, Camp Fire Girls.

"Jaco Building May Be Oldest in Sherman (1856)," Oct. 24, 2012.

"[John B.] McDougall Remembered as Active Throughout Denison Business," Oct. 4, 2012.

"Leader of the Band [Booker T. Ervin] Born in Denison," July 22, 2012.

"Looking at Denison's 'Lost' Structures," Sept. 12, 2012. Waples-Platter Grocers, Educational Institute, Historic DHS, Cotton Mill, St. Xavier's Academy, Security Building, Holden Blacksmithing.

"Looking Back Over Early Part of 20th Century in Grayson County" (Chronology, part 3), Dec. 30, 2012. Key events in Grayson County, 1900–1938, taken from Don Eldredge's 1999 list.

"*Lost Sherman* Book Reveals Treasures of History," Sept. 6, 2012.

"Loy Park Dates Back to 1935, Hosted Campaign Speakers," July 8, 2012.

"Magnetic Faith Healer Comes to Grayson, Lamar Counties," Feb. 29, 2012. Mortimer M. "Snake Editor" Scholl, Dr. Persons.

"McDaniel House [AKA Park Hotel] History Revealing for Denison" (part 1), Oct. 28, 2012. 309 West Crawford St., hotel, guest register, theaters.

"Military Dog Tags of Denison Mayor W.S. Hibbard Found in Colorado," Apr. 25, 2012. Rod and Gun Club.

"More of Denison's Rowdy Days Recalled," Aug. 19, 2012. "Rowdy Joe" Lowe, "Rowdy Kate," horse thieves, Sheriff Lee "Red" Hall.

"More on History of Denison Hotels" (part 2), Nov. 4, 2012. McDaniel House AKA Park Hotel, Ourand Hotel, Palace Hotel, Hotel Denison (first), Hotel Simpson AKA Hotel Denison (second), Alamo Hotel.

"More on the History of Ambrose [Texas]" (part 2), July 3, 2012.

"Old Settlers Association Is Gift That Keeps Giving," Jan. 15, 2012.

"Organizations Formed in Early Days of Denison," Aug. 12, 2012. Fraternal organizations, unions, Vorwaerts Society, music, YMCA, temperance.

"Pioneer Life in Grayson County Remembered," Sept. 16, 2012. 1840s and 1850s, essay by LoRene Madison Taliaferro Reirdon. [NOTE: Corrections to this article on Sept. 27, 2012.]

"Polo Was First Played in America in Denison," May 6, 2012.

"Remembering Some of Our Veterans," Nov. 11, 2012. Dr. John T. Krattiger (DHS Class of 1933).

"Remembering the Ice Houses in Denison," June 6, 2012. Crystal Ice Company, Patrick H. Tobin, home ice delivery.

"Remembering the Meteor's Maiden Journey by Rail," Apr. 12, 2012. Norman C. Dorchester, "Frisco" Railroad, train wreck.

"Right Here in Grayson County, Some Firsts for Texas" (Chronology, part 2), Dec. 20, 2012. Events in Grayson County from 1864 to 1900.

"Rosemary Clooney, Jose Ferrer Eloped in Durant, Spent the Night in [Hotel] Denison," Nov. 28, 2012.

"Sam Rayburn Had His Own Little Excess," Nov. 18, 2012. Speaker of U.S. House of Representatives, 1947 Cadillac.

"Several U.S. Presidents Have Visited the Texoma Area" (part 1), Aug. 1, 2012. Dwight D. Eisenhower, Ulysses S. Grant (Oct. 1874).

"[Sheriff Lee] Red Hall: Keeping Crime Out of Early Denison," Aug. 22, 2012.

"Sherman's Jaco Building Had Long History," May 9, 2012.

"Snapshots of Denison's History in 1876," June 27, 2012. Bunn meat markets, Native Americans, fruit crop, buffalo hides, cement, Methuselah Club, H&TC Railroad, O'Maley, *Sunday Gazetteer.*

"Sophia [Suttonfield Aughinbaugh Coffee Butt] Porter's Garden Revealed Green Thumb," Apr. 15, 2012.

"Sports Teams Shine in Denison's Early Days," Sept. 2, 2012. Hunting, fishing, Tom Dollarhide, baseball, Blue Stockings (1874), Sherman-Denison rivalry, Munson Memorial Park (1887), football begins (1880).

"Story of Olive Ann Oatman [Fairchild] Is Told," Feb. 26, 2012. Kidnapped by Indians, tattoos, married John Fairchild, lived in Sherman TX.

"Tallest Building in Texas Is in Denison, in 1891," Dec. 12, 2012. Leeper Building, Security Building, 331 W. Main St., "Old Stone Face," demolished 1954.

"The Original Old Settlers' [Association] First Gathering," Nov. 7, 2012.

"The Rich History of Delaware Bend [Area]," June 20, 2012.

"The Town of Hagerman Died a Slow Death Making Way for Denison Dam," July 11, 2012.

"There Were Horses Before Fire Trucks," Jan. 4, 2012. First State Bank, First National Bank, Harrison Tone, newspapers, Forest Park, Joseph A. Euper. [NOTE: Herald Democrat archive lists as "Denison Firsts."]

"Thinking Back on Presidents Who Visited Sherman, Denison" (part 2), Aug. 9, 2012. Bob Haney's photographs, Harry S. Truman (1947, 1961), Theodore Roosevelt 1905), Franklin D. Roosevelt (1936), Sam Rayburn's funeral (1961).

"Viaduct Constructed on Austin Street [Avenue] in Denison" (part 2), Jan. 11, 2012. [NOTE: Herald Democrat archive lists as "The Rest of the Denison Viaduct Story."]

"Virginia Point [Methodist] Church to Celebrate 175th Anniversary," Sept. 30, 2012. Oldest continuous Methodist church in North Texas.

"Work on Denison's Viaduct Causes a Look Back to Its History" (part 1), Jan. 8, 2012.

2013

"1892 [May 18] Denison Murder Believed To Be Robbery Gone Wrong" ("Night of Terror," part 2), Oct. 28, 2013.

"1892 [May 18] Murderer Shot His Victim Through the Window" ("Night of Terror," part 4), Nov. 6, 2013.

"20th-Century History Continued, from 1941 to 1980" (Chronology, part 4), Jan. 3, 2013. [Key events in Grayson County.]

"A Discussion of the Liberty [Movie] Theater in Denison," Dec. 8, 2013. James Cuff family, 1927.

"A History of Katy Antique Station [Waples-Platter Grocery]," Feb. 13, 2013. Located at 104 East Main St.

"A Look at Segregated, Integrated Denison Schools," Feb. 6, 2013. Buildings, teachers.

"A Look at the First-Born Residents of Denison," June 21, 2013. Texana Denison McElvany, Denison Nelson, Sam Hanna Jr.

"A Look Back at Nov. 1876 in Denison," July 17, 2013. School, John Nothaf's saddle, Jesse James's mother, lawyers, eagle, *Sunday Gazetteer* (1926), football, hunting.

"A Retail Merchant [W.R. Halton] Selling Pianos and Coffins," Nov. 24, 2013.

"A Texas Feud from 1800s to Present Day," Oct. 16, 2013. Lee-Peacock feud not over.

"Answering Mail, E– or Otherwise, Always Interesting," Sept. 18, 2013. Sugar Bottom barbers, Munson Lake, Orphan Train, Anna Scott, Samuel A. "Po' Sam" Flagg (barbecue), Bells meteorite (1961), Julia Shannon named Sherman streets.

"Beulah Hull Riddle, Daughter of a Confederate Soldier," Mar. 27, 2013. Sherman tornado, Vin Fiz, Grayson County Courthouse.

"Broken 1884 Stone Found Far from Gravesite," July 7, 2013. John B. Francis, Lea Head (researcher), Holloway Cemetery, Vandagriff Monument Company.

"Central Ward School in Denison Remembered," Aug. 28, 2013.

"Checking History Through the *Sunday Gazetteer* [7 Nov. 1926]," July 10, 2013. In 1901: Fire Chief Joe Euper, fire dog "Jeff," Dr. Booth. In 1926: armed mail trains.

"Christmas Eve Holds Special Meaning for Denison," Dec. 22, 2013. First train.

"Dad [Lucious Hord] Remembered on Father's Day," June 16, 2013.

"Denison Church [Trinity Methodist] History Passed on by Relative of Marie [Boren] Trout," May 9, 2013. Rev. Paul O. Cardwell.

"Denison Has Connection to the First President," Sept. 29, 2013. Dr. Laurence A. Washington, Martha D. Washington, Oakwood Cemetery, George I. Patrick, possessions.

"Denison High School Honors Alumni," Sept. 15, 2013. Bredette C. Thomas, Ross Stoddard III, Gregg Watson, Scott Marr, Dr. William Blankenship, Nancy Terry, John Terry, DHS Jazz Ensemble.

"Denison Once Had a Small, But Popular, Airfield [Gray Field]," Feb. 24, 2013. Tom McBee, female pilots, Dr. Don Freeman, Don Bigbee, Raymond Willard Hayes.

"Denison Trivia Remembered," Oct. 9, 2013. Accomplishments of key Denisonians (list).

"Denison, Katy Railroad History Intertwined," Jan. 31, 2013. W.B. Munson Sr., Denison Town Company, Maj. George M. Walker (platted town), histories.

"Denison's Night of Terror [18 May 1892]" (part 1), Oct. 24, 2013.

"Denison's Night of Terror—Third in Series" (part 3), Oct. 30, 2013.

"Doctor [D.H. Bailey] Who Delivered a President [Dwight D. Eisenhower] Remembered," Nov. 27, 2013. Jim Redmon, Jennie Jackson.

"Downtown Sherman [TX] Started Out in a Different Location," May 22, 2013. G.A. Dickerman.

"Following the Moving of the Historic [J.J.] Fairbanks House" (part 1), June 30, 2013.

"Fourteen Added to Terrell High School Hall of Fame," July 21, 2013. Fighting Dragons, school integration, John Clift (sportswriter).

"Frank B. Hughes Shaped Denison Education," Dec. 29, 2013. Superintendent, postmaster.

"Grayson County History Continued, 1981 to Present" (Chronology, part 5), Jan. 6, 2013.

"Grayson County Springs Detailed in Book," Feb. 28, 2013. Gerald Brune, *Springs of Texas.*

"Historic [J.J.] Fairbanks House Flourishes After Move" (part 2), July 3, 2013. John Henry Kirk.

"History Made in the Air Touches Local Areas," Jan. 27, 2013. Vin Fiz (first plane over Denison, 1911).

"Ice Storms Throughout Past Years," Dec. 11, 2013. Blizzard of 1899, ice storms (1945, 1949).

"In the News When Ike Was Born 123 Years Ago [14 Oct. 1890]," Oct. 13, 2013. Events reported in newspaper; circus animal escapes.

"Information on Denison Poet [LaUna de Cordova Skinner] Leads to Other Findings," Apr. 7, 2013. Daughters of the Republic of Texas, Gen. Sidney Sherman.

"Information on Early Schools in Denison," Feb. 20, 2013. Educational Institute, Sherman school for ex-slaves, Justin Raynal, Central Ward Elementary School, Abner Ragsdale.

"Jacobs Well [Mineral Resort] Was Once Strong Draw for Denison," Aug. 11, 2013.

"Learning to Play the Piano—Or at Least Trying To," Nov. 13, 2013. Lula Mae Hays, Bebe Bodamer, Judge R.C. Vaughan, Tommy Loy, Little Symphony Orchestra.

"Letter [1 Nov. 1943] to World War II Soldiers Kept Boys Informed," Oct. 20, 2013. Judge R.C. Vaughan, *Denison Herald* newsletter, Tropical Gardens nightclub.

"[Mavis Anne] Bryant Wrote Photography Book Without Photos," Mar. 31, 2013. 125 photographers who worked in Denison.

"Mayor [Alex W.] Acheson Brought Denison National Attention," Nov. 17, 2013. Unpaid taxes, Red River navigation. [NOTE: Herald Democrat archive lists as "Mayor Acheson's Big Idea."]

"Memories of Central Ward School, Teachers," Sept. 25, 2013.

"Mystery of Missing [Denison] Gate Solved," Sept. 1, 2013. Exhibit at World Cotton Centennial (1884-85), later at Exposition Hall, destroyed in fire (Aug. 1893).

"North Texas Baptist College [and Seminary] Recalled," Feb. 10, 2013. Education for African Americans.

"Notes About Early Denison Residents," Mar. 10, 2013. Town's first year: jail, city hall, Board of Trade.

"Old Photo Leads to Research of [Elmer E. Davis] Motor Company," May 26, 2013.

"Orphan Train Brought Children to Texas for New Lives," Aug. 15, 2013.

"Photo [of Municipal Swimming Pool] Conjures Memories of an Earlier Time in Sherman," Apr. 4, 2013. Denison's Barrett Building, Louis Carlat.

"Picture [1936] Shows Employees of Denison Cotton Mill," Jan. 13, 2013.

"Recreation of [1956] Yellow Jacket Boat Trip Planned for 2016," Sept. 4, 2013.

"Riverside Park Prank [Shooting] Lends Interest to Story of History," July 24, 2013. Map.

"Samuel A. Flagg (Po' Sam), the Legend," Aug. 21, 2013. Colbert OK, barbecue, died 1985.

"St. Patrick's Day 1896 Was Major Celebration in Denison," Mar. 17, 2013. St. Patrick's Catholic Church, Ancient Order of Hibernians, High Mass, parade, banquet.

"Steamboat 'Annie Peruna' Built in Denison," Mar. 13, 2013. Parody, Sugar Bottom, Red River.

"Tex O'Reilly's Adventurous Life Began in Denison," Feb. 13, 2013. Journalist, soldier of fortune, Dr. Alexander W. Acheson.

"The Day [John F.] Kennedy Was Killed [Nov. 22, 1963]," Nov. 21, 2013.

"The Famous Doc Holliday Likely to Have Practiced Dentistry in Denison," Aug. 1, 2013.

"The Gate of Denison, Gate City of Texas," May 16, 2013. Exhibit at World Cotton Centennial (1884-85, New Orleans), women's artwork.

"The White Pig Stand Fondly Remembered," Aug. 18, 2013. Carl McCraw, carhops, drive-in restaurants.

"U.S. Presidents, First Lady, Visit Sherman-Denison Area," Mar. 7, 2013. Eleanor Roosevelt (1936, 1940), William Howard Taft, first church services in Sherman.

"Unity Church Founder Had Denison Ties," Aug. 8, 2013. Charles and Myrtle Fillmore, tuberculosis treatment; Roy Rogers Museum, Bob Young.

"*USS Texas* Had Denison Connection," June 23, 2013. Adm. Adolphus Andrews, Berenice Platter Andrews, Waples-Platter Grocer Company.

"Viaduct Flags a Source of Pride," Oct. 6, 2013. Four viaducts.

"White Elephant Livery Stable Important Denison Business," Nov. 10, 2013. 121 N. Rusk Ave. at Woodard, Jeremiah H. "Jerry" Nolan, John L. Higginson Sr.

"White Rock [Public] School Absorbed into the Sherman School District," May 1, 2013.

2014

"1984 Yellow Jackets Inducted into the Denison Sports Hall of Fame," Oct. 12, 2014.

"A History of the Grayson County Poor Farm," Apr. 20, 2014. Dusty Williams, Edna Gladney.

"A Look at Businesses of Denison's Past [1895]," Apr. 23, 2014. A.B. Hobson, George H. Crank.

"A Presidential Delivery Is Made in Denison," Oct. 22, 2014. Dwight D. Eisenhower, Dr. Daniel H. Bailey.

"A Storyteller Spins Tales About Women in Denison," Aug. 6, 2014. Mortimer M. "Snake Editor" Scholl, Belle Starr, *Historic Denison*.

"A Walk Through the City of Crape Myrtles," July 9, 2014. 1938 planting campaign, Jennie Jackson, Texas Nursery, Sam and Herby Roy, Texas State Shrub, Paris TX.

"Bloomfield Academy [Okla.] Boarded Native Americans for Decades Near Red River," Aug. 13, 2014.

"Book [*Journey to Freedom*] Chronicles Life of Black Family in Denison," Feb. 9, 2014. Lonnie R. Bunkley. [NOTE: For corrections to this article, see Feb. 26, 2014.]

"Child's Birth Put Denison on the Map," Oct. 15, 2014. Dwight D. Eisenhower.

"Circus Dreams Come True," Aug. 20, 2014. Gainesville TX Community Circus, stars, zoo.

"Denison Has History of Education for Black Students," Feb. 23, 2014. Schools: Anderson, North Texas Baptist College and Seminary, Burleson, Terrell, Langston, Walton, Wims.

"Denison Has Long History of Bad Guys," Mar. 16, 2014. W.E. Koop, "Rowdy Joe" Lowe, "Rowdy Kate," Rock Jack Norton, Hurricane Bill. [NOTE: Herald Democrat archive lists as "Denison's History of Bad Guys."]

"Denison Music Through the Years Offers Variety," Mar. 30, 2014.

"Denison Telephones Make History in 1956," May 7, 2014. Two companies (1886–1918). [NOTE: Herald Democrat archive lists as "Denison's Telephonic History Discussed."]

"Denison Women Had a Leg Up on Hosiery in Early 1900s," Feb. 20,

2014. Gate City Hosiery Mill founded ca. 1900.

"Denison-Born Leader of D-Day Remembered," June 4, 2014. Dwight D. Eisenhower, Johnny Goldston.

"Denison: I Remember When," Mar. 2, 2014. Article by Elizabeth Bledsoe, teacher (1986).

"Denison's First Red Cross Canteen Recalled," Apr. 30, 2014. World War I, World War II.

"Denison's More Colorful Residents Discussed," Mar. 26, 2014. Judge Mortimer M. "Snake Editor" Scholl, Dr. H.T. Walker, pranks.

"Denison's Overpasses Serve Residents for Decades," Apr. 3, 2014. Crawford Street double underpass (built 1914), school sanitary connections (1912). [NOTE: Herald Democrat archive lists as "Denison Overpass Remembered."]

"Denison's 'Skyscraper' [Security Building] and Bank Buildings from Its History," Mar. 13, 2014.

"Denison's Volunteer Cavalry, Rode with 'Rough Riders'," Jan. 8, 2014. Denison Rifles AKA Troop L, First Regiment, Texas Cavalry Volunteers, Lt. Isaac N. Layne.

"Dr. Pepper Bottling Company in Denison Recalled," Apr. 27, 2014. Also Red River Bottling Works, City Bottling, Birely Soda, 7-Up Bottling, Coca-Cola.

"Dream Jobs and First Jobs," Aug. 3, 2014. Ashburn's Ice Cream.

"Early Law Enforcement Liked to Mix It Up Every Now and Then," May 4, 2014. Mortimer M. "Snake Editor" Scholl, *Historic Denison*, Lee "Red" Hall, "Carriage Point," covered wagon caravans.

"Early Newspapers in Texoma Remembered," June 11, 2014. [NOTE: Herald Democrat archive lists as "Early Newspaper Discussed."]

"Famous Guests of the Denison Hotel," Oct. 19, 2014.

"Former Denisonian [Nat Floyd] Remembered in 'Expendables' from 1945," Dec. 15, 2014.

"Gasoline Tax Goes Back to 1927," Oct. 8, 2014. Messenger's Chapel UMC bell stolen.

"Grayson County's Prison on Wheels Housed Chain Gangs," Mar. 23, 2014. [NOTE: Herald Democrat archive lists as "Jail on Wheels."]

"Heroes Abound in the History of Denison," May 15, 2014. Earl G. Thurman Jr. (Bataan), Carnegie Hero Medalists, Capt. Chesley B. "Sully" Sullenberger.

"Historic [Simpson/Denison] Hotel Building Remembered," Oct. 29, 2014.

"Hook-and-Ladder Truck Served Denison [Fire Department] for 40 Years," Jan. 12, 2014. Three major fires.

"I Remember When," June 25, 2014. Musings: telephones, election night, typewriters, corner grocery stores, food, Loy Lake.

"In Honor of Some of Texas' Oldest Citizens," June 8, 2014. Lou Harris (oldest woman in Grayson County, 1936); Helen A. Morrison Cummins (second oldest), Amy J. Barns.

"In Honor of Texas Women and Their Drums," June 29, 2014. Author Angela Smith, Helen Cole.

"Katy Onion Soup Helped Develop the Katy as a Place of Comfort," Jan. 22, 2014. [NOTE: Herald Democrat archive lists as "Onion Soup Katy Style."]

"Kentuckytown [Texas] —A Once Thriving Community," Jan. 1, 2014.

"Kentuckytown Hangings Started with Robbery Attempt" (part 1), Nov. 15, 2014.

"Letters from a House of Representatives Member [Vernon Beckham]," June 18, 2014. Tom B. Anderson, Red River houseboat trip (1910), Denison Live Wires (1911), Crawford Street double underpass (1914), Munson Park, "Fort Acheson."

"Literary Agent [Annie Laurie Williams] from Denison Remembered," Sept. 3, 2014.

"Little Bits of Denison History Very Interesting," Mar. 20, 2014. John B. McDougall, Tex O'Reilly, pecan tree bank, first fire (1873), first twins (1876), gas vs. electricity.

"Local [German] Prisoner of War Camp Remembered," July 30, 2014.

"Local Woman's [Billie Letts] Writing Career Reached Far Beyond the Local Area," Aug. 24, 2014.

"Locals Celebrated as Part of Black History Month," Feb. 12, 2014. JoAnn Perkins, Clora Bryant, Dr. Claude Organ, Marguerite Bradshaw. [NOTE: Herald Democrat archive lists as "Black History Month Offers Time to Celebrate Locals."]

"Memories of Growing Up in the 1930s," Feb. 2, 2014. Author Rusty Williams, Colbert OK, Red River Bridge War, Red River Bottoms, rural electrification.

"More on Entertainment in Early Days in Denison" (part 2), July 23, 2014. Rendezvous Club, Tropical Gardens, Swiss Village, Olan Atherton.

"Movie 'Monuments Men' Might Remind Some of Local Quedlinburg Tie," Feb. 17, 2014. Joe T. Meador, theft of treasures, World War II, Whitewright TX. [NOTE: Herald Democrat archive lists as "George Clooney's 'Monuments Men' Might Remind Some of Local Quedlinburg Tie."]

"Notes on Notable Denisonians of Past in Celebration of Black History Month," Feb. 26, 2014. Claude Robert Platte Jr., Booker T. Ervin

II, Helen P. Cole, Sgt. Marva Lewis. [NOTE: Herald Democrat archive lists as "Denisonians of the Past Noted in Celebration of Black History Month."]

"Perrin Air Force Base Museum Continues to Grow and Change," June 15, 2014. Rabbit hunting.

"Populist Party's 'Joan of Arc' [Mary Elizabeth Lease] Got Her Start at Temperance Meeting in Denison," Sept. 2, 2014.

"Posse Takes Justice into Its Own Hands" (Kentuckytown, part 2), Nov. 15, 2014.

"Presidential Visits to Denison," Apr. 16, 2014. Ulysses S. Grant (1874), Theodore Roosevelt (1905), Franklin D. Roosevelt (1936).

"Recalling the Sounds of Zoe Ella Rutherford," May 29, 2014. Charlsie Rutherford Budd (sister), DHS grads, musicians, World War II. [NOTE: Zoe Ella was the first woman pilot to receive her license at Denison's Gray Field.]

"Remembering Denison's Entertainment District" (part 1), July 20, 2014. Betty Jane Hickey Brodie, life on Bullock Street, Oak View Inn, Tom Mix Circus, Stork Club, Tick Tock Dinner Club, Oasis Club, Orchard Club, Snug Harbor, Sand Spring, "Whippet" car.

"Remembering Denison's West End," Dec. 16, 2014.

"Robbers Buried Under the Tree on Which They Were Hanged" (Kentuckytown, part 3), Nov. 15, 2014.

"Sears Street History Deeper Than Just a Name Change," Sept. 27, 2014. Formerly called Leon Street.

"Soda Fountains, Book Stores, Ice Cream and Soda Bottling," Nov. 19, 2014. Thomas L. Reber.

"Sophia [Suttonfield Aughinbaugh Coffee Butt] Porter's Gardens Showed Her Green Thumb," Apr. 9, 2014. Glen Eden.

"Sorting Out This and That About Denison," Jan. 15, 2014. Deer Park Swimming Pool (1916), crape myrtles vs. roses.

"Springs of Health Possess 'Curative Properties'," Mar. 9, 2014. Oil springs, Rock Bluff on Red River, Jacobs Well Resort.

"Tales of the Sinking of the *Sultana*," July 17, 2014. C.M. Eldredge, Civil War vet, survived *Sultana* explosion in Mississippi River.

"Talk of [Sand Springs/Waterloo] Cave Brings Up Many Memories of Locals," Dec. 7, 2014.

"Texoma's Outlaw History," Oct. 26, 2014. John B. McDougall, Jesse James, Cole Younger.

"The First Meeting of the Old Settlers," Nov. 5, 2014.

"The Girl with the Blue Tattoo [Olive Ann Oatman Fairchild] and Other Bits of Denison History," Nov. 2, 2014.

"The Greatest Night To Be a Yellow Jacket," Dec. 21, 2014. Football championship.

"The Life and Times of Bertie Eloise Newsom," Jan. 29, 2014. Thomas Wall, adopted girl who died at age 13, Sherman TX.

"This Is Not Texoma's First Dance with Old Man Winter Blues," Mar. 6, 2014. Blizzard of 1899, ice storms (1945, 1949). [NOTE: Herald Democrat archive lists as "2014 Not Texoma's Only Tango with Old Man Winter Blues."]

"Train Robberies Weren't Just for Western Novels," Jan. 19, 2014. Katy train robberies (1901 and 1921).

"True Love Will Out," July 27, 2014. Harrison Tone Jr. eventually marries Frederica Cobb; Tone Abstract Company.

"Uncovering Denison's Colorful Past in Downtown," Aug. 26, 2014. 307 W. Main St., Esler's Paint & Paper Co. (sign), White Elephant Saloon.

Books

Frontier Denison, Texas. Edited by Mavis Anne Bryant. Charleston SC: CreateSpace, 2015.

Images of America: Denison. Co-authored with Mavis Anne Bryant. Images of America Series. Mount Pleasant SC: Arcadia Publishing, 2011.

Two Schools on Main Street: The Pride of Denison, Texas, 1873–2007. Co-authored with Mavis Anne Bryant. Denison TX: Gate City Publishing, 2009.

Website of Denison Alumni Association

"1909 Alumni Association Minutes Found."

"1953 DHS Band Trip to Washington, D.C."

"A Soldier [Casey Hunt] Returns Home."

"A Spanish Veni, Vidi, Vici."

"Alice Kinney Cox Story."

"An Evening with Marva Lewis."

"Ashburn's Ice Cream."

"Billy Holcomb and the Bordertown Gospel Band, Circa 1984."

"Black History Month Offers Time to Celebrate Locals."

"Bob Cherry, Class of 1942, Golden Gloves Champion in Denison."

"Bobby G. Mathews, Class of 1954."

"C. J. Ransom, Class of 1958."

"Central Ward School."

"Clora Bryant, Class of 1943."

"Danna Burns Harvey, Class of 1960, Artist."
"Dee Gaines, Class of 1952."
"Denison's Hometown Heroes Celebration," June 6, 2009.
"Denison's Ice Houses."
"DHS Teachers Remembered." Elizabeth Bledsoe, Maggie Sommerville.
"Donis Kay McBee, Class of 1953."
"Durham's Hamburgers."
"Edward Butler, Class of 1949." Terrell High School.
"Eisenhower Auditorium Dedicated."
"Elementary School Remembrances."
"Elvis, Gone but Not Forgotten." Gerry Ford.
"Frontier Village Stirs Memories."
"Gil (Sonny) Stricklin, Class of 1953."
"'Girls' Morning Out' Group Takes Train Trip."
"Jack Maguire, Hometown Writer" (from *Denison Post*).
"Jim Sears and the Flopped Pictures."
"Joel Ward's 'Porch It.'"
"Justin Raynal, Denison Benefactor."
"Memories of Grocery Stores."
"Mystery of the Y-Teen Cup."
"Neil Shirley, First Full-Time DHS Band Director."
"Nondas [Baxley] Meets Nondas."
"Number One Cowboy Fan" [Billy Holcomb].
"Olan Taul, Class of 1956."
"Pictures from the Past."
"Remember Slanguage?"
"Remembering Downtown Denison in the Fifties."
"Remembering the Hive in Denison."
"Remembrances of Miss Elizabeth Bledsoe."
"Revisiting the Denison Barber Shop."
"Sam Houston School."
"The Books [*Two Schools on Main Street*] Have Arrived!"
"The Katy Railroad."
"The Story of 'Little Pat'."
"The White Pig Stand."
"Tommy Loy, Class of 1947."
"Traditions, Fall 2005."
"UFO Sighting in Denison, Texas."
"Under the Colors (Dated Sept. 5, 1943)."
"Viaduct Flags a Source of Pride."
"We're the Best Forevermore, Senior Class of '64!"
"Yesterday—Little Stores."

Miscellaneous Writings

"A New Town in Texas Gets a School House." Speech, 2008.

"Brief History of Grayson County Frontier Village." Aug. 9, 2007.

"Denison Trivia."

"Early Day Elite, Commoners Found Fun Spots in Grayson County." *Texoma Living Magazine*, Summer 2008.

"Fannin's Best-Kept Secret Goes Public."

"I Remember When."

"Judge Jake Loy." *Texoma Living Magazine*, June 2007.

"Red Store Story." Press release, Eisenhower Birthplace, June 13, 2005.

"Sophia [Suttonfield Aughinbaugh Coffee Butt] Porter and Her Garden." Speech to Sherman Garden Club, Mar. 11, 2005.

"The Mayor of Cookie Town." *Texoma Living Magazine*, Winter 2007. [NOTE: *Texoma Living Online* erroneously attributes this article to Edward Southerland.]

"Tribute to Dr. Lawrence Augustine Washington Jr."

"Woodmen Circle Home." Speech, Sept. 25, 2010.

Fig. 31. Donna and David Hunt celebrate fiftieth wedding anniversary, 2015. Photo by Quin Studio.

Made in the USA
Charleston, SC
17 August 2015